THE SOCIAL REALITY OF EUROPE
AFTER THE CRISIS

About Policy Network

Policy Network is an international thinktank and research institute. Its network spans national borders across Europe and the wider world with the aim of promoting the best progressive thinking on the major social and economic challenges of the 21st century.

Our work is driven by a network of politicians, policymakers, business leaders, public service professionals, and academic researchers who work on long-term issues relating to public policy, political economy, social attitudes, governance and international affairs. This is complemented by the expertise and research excellence of Policy Network's international team.

A platform for research and ideas

- Promoting expert ideas and political analysis on the key economic, social and political challenges of our age.
- Disseminating research excellence and relevant knowledge to a wider public audience through interactive policy networks, including interdisciplinary and scholarly collaboration.
- Engaging and informing the public debate about the future of European and global progressive politics.

A network of leaders, policymakers and thinkers

- Building international policy communities comprising individuals and affiliate institutions.
- Providing meeting platforms where the politically active, and potential leaders of the future, can engage with each other across national borders and with the best thinkers who are sympathetic to their broad aims.
- Engaging in external collaboration with partners including higher education institutions, the private sector, thinktanks, charities, community organisations, and trade unions.
- Delivering an innovative events programme combining in-house seminars with large-scale public conferences designed to influence and contribute to key public debates.

www.policy-network.net

About the Foundation for European Progressive Studies (FEPS)

FEPS is the first progressive political foundation established at the European level. Created in 2007 and co-financed by the European parliament, it aims at establishing an intellectual crossroad between social democracy and the European project. It puts fresh thinking at the core of its action and serves as an instrument for pan-European intellectual and political reflection.

Acting as a platform for ideas, FEPS relies first and foremost on a network of members composed of more than 40 national political foundations and thinktanks from all over the EU. The foundation also closely collaborates with a number of international correspondents and partners in the world that share the ambition to foster research, promote debate and spread progressive thinking.

www.feps-europe.eu

THE SOCIAL REALITY OF EUROPE AFTER THE CRISIS

Trends, Challenges and Responses

Patrick Diamond, Roger Liddle and Daniel Sage

}{ policy network

FOUNDATION FOR EUROPEAN
PROGRESSIVE STUDIES
FONDATION EUROPÉENNE
D'ÉTUDES PROGRESSISTES

ROWMAN &
LITTLEFIELD
INTERNATIONAL

London • New York

Published by Rowman & Littlefield International Ltd.
Unit A, Whitacre, 26-34 Stannary Street, London, SE11 4AB
www.rowmaninternational.com

Rowman & Littlefield International Ltd. is an affiliate of Rowman & Littlefield
4501 Forbes Boulevard, Suite 200, Lanham, Maryland 20706, USA
With additional offices in Boulder, New York, Toronto (Canada), and Plymouth (UK)
www.rowman.com

British Library Cataloguing in Publication Data
A catalogue record for this book is available from the British Library

ISBN: PB 978-1-78348-538-3

Library of Congress Control Number: 2015940889

ISBN 978-1-78348-538-3 (pbk. : alk. paper)
ISBN 978-1-78348-539-0 (electronic)

♾™ The paper used in this publication meets the minimum requirements
of American National Standard for Information Sciences—Permanence of Paper
for Printed Library Materials, ANSI/NISO Z39.48-1992.

Printed in the United States of America

CONTENTS

ACKNOWLEDGEMENTS

This pamphlet would not have been possible without the generous support of the Foundation for European Progressive Studies (FEPS). In particular, we would like to thank Ernst Stetter and Ania Skrzypek, who provided intellectual inspiration as well as practical assistance. Solidar kindly hosted a conference in the European parliament at which the social situation in Europe was discussed with leading experts in the field. We would also like to thank our colleagues at Policy Network for their dedication and professionalism in preparing this report, especially Ben Dilks, Robert Philpot and Renaud Thillaye.

Patrick Diamond, Roger Liddle and Daniel Sage

INTRODUCTION

The economic crisis that has unfolded since 2008 has had, and continues to have, a profound effect on the lives of Europe's citizens. Economically, politically and socially, the crisis has led to fundamental changes in many EU member states. This report seeks to examine the new 'social reality' of post-crisis Europe. In essence it describes how a profound divergence of experience between north and south challenges previous assumptions that European integration would drive a seemingly automatic process of convergence. Altogether, we identify four separate dynamic forces that have the potential to reshape Europe's social reality in the coming years. First, the most explicit effects of the crisis have been felt across *economies and labour markets*, with Europe's relative economic performance analysed and compared in the first section. Second, there is much debate about the effects of the crisis on Europe's poorest citizens, particularly in relation to *poverty and inequality*, the issues that dominate section two of the report. Third, the EU has set ambitious targets for progress in education, while the effects of the crisis on health have been much discussed; there are ongoing debates about the sustainability of existing systems of public service provision, specifically *education and health*. These challenges are assessed in the third part of the report. In the fourth section of the report, the *political and cultural* makeup of post-crisis Europe is examined, with unsettling implications for Europe's political class.

The divergence this report describes has taken place against the backdrop of trends and developments already in train long before the crisis hit. The process of deindustrialisation and the associated decline of employment in manufacturing industry has been wrought by technological change, a global shift in economic power from west to east and rising consumer demands for services. These long-term, structural trends across most EU member states have contributed to the rise of more precarious work arrangements and the strengthening of 'insider' and 'outsider' divisions in labour markets. Moreover, the implementation of policies today associated with 'crisis' austerity programmes such as benefit conditionality, employment activation, higher retirement ages and reductions in benefit entitlements are not 'new' policies in European welfare states. They have been part of the reform landscape of Europe since the late 1990s. Such policies were pioneered before the eurozone crisis in countries such as Germany, Sweden and the UK, with new recruits – such as Italy and Spain – now following suit. This interplay between policy change and more fundamental, structural forces has influenced debates about the future of Europe since before the crisis, with calls for a 'new' welfare state or social model for Europe, achieving their strongest political expression through the launch of the Lisbon agenda in 1999.[1] As well as creating new challenges, the crisis has accentuated the impact of pre-existing trends, raising profound questions about the sustainability and success of the European model.

So while old problems are being aggravated in European societies, new problems are emerging.[2] While Europe has never had, nor necessarily aspired to create, a uniform social model,[3] and the enlargement of the union has only served to expand the varieties of European 'welfare capitalism'. Yet for all this diversity, the common pre-crisis assumption of converging social standards and economic growth has been shattered. The Lisbon strategy assumed that the 'European social model', despite its distinctive national variants with their own institutional path dependency, faced common challenges that the EU could help address by laying down common principles of action and reform. The impact of the crisis has also called this previous assumption into question. A Europe of diverging regions is increasingly evident, as old ambitions of a European-wide convergence in prosperity have ground to a halt. Partly as a consequence, migration from struggling states to richer ones has intensified. Public concerns about the social and economic impact of more rapid migration have intensified debate about the viability of multiculturalism and the prospects of more integrated societies. Prospering in this more insecure and politically unstable Europe are the populist parties: whether from the left, as in Greece and Spain, or the right, as in France and the UK.

This report offers a broad overview of key trends in structural divergence. Other developments such as patterns of gender inequality and the life chances of ethnic minority groups are not considered, but remain of vital importance. Throughout, the report charts the social, economic and political forces remaking the new, post-crisis Europe. Ultimately, the intention is to better understand the challenges facing the EU and its member states. This is necessary if economic competitiveness, inclusive prosperity, social sustainability and political cohesion are to be restored.

NOTES

1. See Esping-Andersen, G. (2002), *Why We Need a New Welfare State,* Oxford: Oxford University Press.
2. See Social Protection Committee (2014), *Social Europe: Aiming for Inclusive Growth – Annual Report of the Social Protection Committee,* Brussels: European Commission.
3. See Esping-Andersen, G. (1990), *The Three Worlds of Welfare Capitalism,* Cambridge: Polity Press. In it, he outlined his influential thesis of the different 'worlds of welfare capitalism', challenging the notion of a single European model and homogeneous road to prosperity. Esping-Andersen argued that Europe had three distinct models of welfare capitalism: liberal, corporate-conservative and social democratic. The UK, Germany and Sweden are often taken as the respective archetypes for each 'welfare regime'.

ECONOMIES AND LABOUR MARKETS

ECONOMIC GROWTH

Although the most serious risks of the economic crisis such as a complete breakdown of the eurozone have seemingly now been averted (although at the time of writing, a Greek exit remains distinctly plausible), many European states nevertheless continue to endure anaemic economic growth and seemingly chronic structural weaknesses. In November 2014, the European commission significantly downgraded its forecasts for growth in the eurozone. In its February 2015 forecast, the commission pointed to 'new developments . . . that are expected to brighten in the near term the EU's economic outlook that would have otherwise deteriorated'. Predicted growth for the eurozone is now expected to rise from a sluggish 0.8 per cent in 2014 to 1.3 per cent in 2015 and 1.9 per cent in 2016. Crucially, Germany – the economic engine of the eurozone – has predicted growth of 1.5 per cent in 2015 and two per cent in 2016. This modest trend towards the return of to growth is put down to the decline in oil prices, the depreciation of the euro, the European Central Bank's (ECB) embrace of a large-scale quantitative easing programme, and the commission's own InvestEU investment plan. However, even on this more optimistic outlook, the commission still expects unemployment in the eurozone to average 10.6 per cent in 2016 and 9.3 per cent in the EU as a whole: this is considerably above the pre-crisis levels of 7.5 per cent and 7.2 per cent respectively.[1] Even in Germany, which has been the EU's greatest success story in terms of employment growth, the modest prospects of growth feed fears of a 'German illusion', the phrase coined by the economist Marcel Fratzscher to describe Germany's apparent economic weaknesses and underlying vulnerabilities.[2] In short, Fratzscher argues that Germany's economic strength has been embellished by factors such as its labour market performance, with deep weaknesses in other areas of the economy, such as a comparatively low rate of domestic investment and a rapidly ageing population. On the other hand, Germany is increasingly at the centre of a cluster of countries such as Austria, the Czech Republic, Poland, Slovakia and Romania that excel in manufacturing and are where Europe's industrial jobs are increasingly located.[3] This shift in the pattern of manufacturing and supply chains has been a factor in the challenges of declining competitiveness and social sustainability that southern Europe faces.

The overall figures for the EU and the eurozone conceal vast differences in predicted economic performance. For instance, after years of sluggish growth and a 'double-dip' recession, Ireland and the UK are predicted to enjoy robust growth in 2016: 4.6 per cent in Ireland and 2.7 per cent in the UK. Nevertheless, claims of a resurgence of success in the UK in particular should be treated cautiously.

Despite the gradual re-emergence of UK growth over the last 18 months (in part a bounce-back against the calamitous drop in output immediately after the financial crisis), and the strong growth in employment, a long-term view of economic performance indicates a deeper trend of relative UK decline compared to the major economies of continental Europe. In the years before the crisis among the four big EU economies – the UK economy had caught up with France and Germany, which had previously enjoyed the highest GDP per person levels in purchasing power standard (PPS).[4]

By 2005, the UK had a GDP per person PPS of 27,800: higher than Germany (26,000), France (24,700) and Italy (22,400). By 2013,

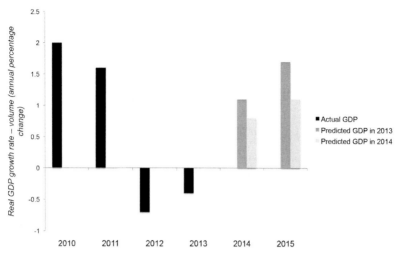

Figure 2.1 Actual and predicted GDP in the eurozone: 2010–15. *Source*: European commission.

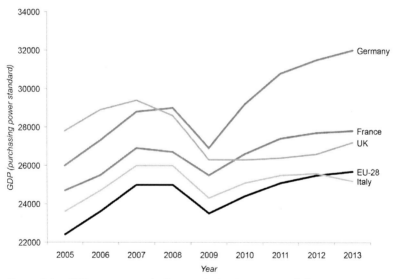

Figure 2.2 GDP per person in France, Italy, Germany and the UK: 2005–13. *Source*: Eurostat. *Note*: GDP per person in purchasing power standard.

however, the UK stood at 27,200. This was some way behind that of Germany (32,000) and even France (27,800), a trend that might seem surprising given the portrayal of the French economy as a 'basket case' by sections of the UK political and media establishment. That the economic crisis has driven new trends in GDP growth in Europe is evident in the experiences of other countries in the EU. As Figure 2.3 indicates, the three northern European countries of Denmark, the Netherlands and Sweden enjoyed steadily rising GDP per person PPS growth between 2005 and 2013. Equally in eastern-central Europe, the Czech Republic and Poland have continued to thrive economically. In particular, Polish growth has been remarkable: from a GDP per person PPS of 11,500 to 17,500 in eight years. This is part of the Polish 'economic miracle'; in 2009, when the EU was in the darkest nadir of the crisis, Poland was the only EU economy that continued to experience economic growth. The EU's 'convergence machine' is still alive and well to Germany's east.

As such, Poland's real GDP is now almost 20 per cent higher than in 2008, while the rest of the EU is only recently making up its losses from when the financial crisis first broke. Where those

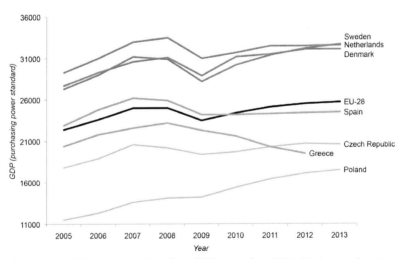

Figure 2.3   GDP per person in selected EU countries: 2005–13. *Source*: Eurostat.
Note: GDP per person in purchasing power standard.

losses have been most severe is also shown in Figure 2.3: Greece, where GDP per person was *lower* in 2012 compared to 2005, and Spain, where by 2013 there was a rise of just 1,600 (and a loss of 1,700 since 2007, the high point of Spanish GDP). The scale of this divergence is illustrated in Figure 2.4, which shows the average GDP per person change between 2005 and 2013 across the EU's seven distinct regions.[5] Average change has been greatest in the Baltic region (6,000) but with relatively strong growth of over 4,000 PPS in the continental, Nordic, east-central and south-eastern regions. In contrast, the southern member states have collectively experienced a rise in GDP per person of only 1,633 since the crisis. The UK and Ireland fared the worst, however, with an overall joint contraction of 150, underlining their unusual degree of exposure to the financial services sector.

This picture is seemingly at odds with the economic progress apparently enjoyed by the UK in the past two years. However, while the UK has recently experienced some of the strongest economic growth in the EU, with 2.6 per cent growth in the last year[6] and a buoyant labour market,[7] its poor performance on living standards reflects the unique experience of the UK during the crisis. This includes a significantly sharper fall in GDP during 2008–09 compared to other countries, an over-dependence on financial services, the depreciation of sterling against the euro, and the apparent transition of the UK from a pre-crisis economy of high employment and high wages to a post-crisis economy of high employment and low wages, reflecting weak productivity growth and, throughout periods, strong net migration expanding the workforce. As the ONS observes, before 2008 the UK had the highest growth in wages in the G7; in the post-crisis world, however, the UK now has the lowest wages among the industrialised countries.[8] Living standards have begun to improve in recent months as nominal wages outstrip the unusually low inflation rate, but the disparity in the UK's economic performance – between high growth and stagnant living standards – is an important feature of political debate in the UK which shows little sign of abating. In February 2015, for example, the Institute for Fiscal Studies confirmed that the incomes of working-age people in the UK were yet to rise above pre-crisis levels in 2007–08.[9] The over-65s have done better.

Another dimension of the post-crisis economy in Europe is the exacerbation of regional inequalities. Europe now has an arc of wealth growing through the centre of the continent to Scandinavia and south-east England and touching north-east Spain and northern Italy. Regional differences within many states are pronounced, however, most notably in Italy, Spain and the UK. In 2011, regional GDP per person (PPS) in Britain ranged from 80,400 in Inner London to 16,100 in West Wales and the Valleys. Furthermore, the gap between the two regions has grown since the start of the last decade. Other deprived regions in the UK have similarly experienced a decline in GDP since before the crisis, most notably Cornwall, Northern Ireland and the Tees Valley.

In short, the distribution of economic growth in Europe looks startlingly different in 2013 compared to 2005. Some regions, such as the northern and central-eastern countries, are considerably richer per inhabitant. Others, most notably the south of Europe and the

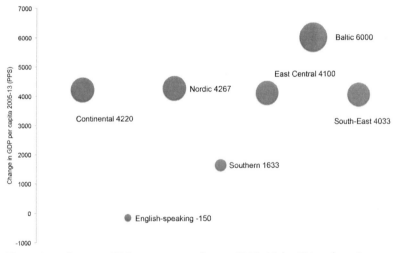

Figure 2.4 Average GDP per person change 2005–13 by EU region. *Source:* Eurostat. *Note:* GDP per person in purchasing power standard.

English-speaking countries, have fared much worse. Many of these poor performers have deep-seated weaknesses in intermediate skills. Ireland, Spain and the UK have had to cope with the after-effects of property booms that collapsed. Underlying this shift are deep structural trends that pre-existed the financial crisis, not least the growing disconnection between the southern member states and manufacturing production chains in the industrial heartlands of Europe, as the accession countries in the east provide more accessible, low-cost labour.[10]

INCOMES

Europe has always been a union comprised of economic unequals, but the section above indicates a sharpening of these inequalities over time, especially between the robust performance of the northern continental states and the experience of the poorer member states along the Mediterranean. Although the wider ambition of European convergence still seems a credible goal for the rapidly expanding eastern European countries, the prospect of those in the south – which, with their rapid economic and income growth in the 1990s and 2000s, appeared to represent the realisation of European convergence – have now declined.

Alongside GDP, changes in incomes further underline the new social reality of post-crisis Europe. Table 2.5 shows evidence of the great stagnation in British living standards, with median net equivalised incomes (PPS) falling from 16,894 in 2005 to 16,469 in 2013. Such figures give credence to the centre-left critique in the UK: that

Table 2.5 Median incomes in France, Germany, Italy and the UK: 2005–13[11]

	2005	2006	2007	2008	2009	2010	2011	2012	2013
FR	14,503	14,981	15,149	17,493	17,741	17,782	18,161	18,784	19,384
DE	15,651	15,167	17,325	18,007	17,954	17,573	18,395	19,208	19,371
IT	13,680	13,871	14,401	15,262	15,198	15,206	15,781	15,575	15,342
UK	16,894	17,630	18,778	18,543	16,819	15,869	15,776	16,447	16,469

Source: Eurostat. Note: Median equivalised net incomes.

despite robust economic and employment growth in recent years, living standards have remained stagnant for almost a decade and that this is not a recovery that is significantly touching the lives of ordinary citizens. This is in stark contrast to the continued increase in median incomes in both France and Germany, while even Italy has experienced some income growth, albeit at a significantly slower rate. The impact of the crisis has seen the UK lose its position as the most prosperous of the major economies: UK living standards are now more on par with Italy than either France or Germany.

Yet the starkest divergence in living standards is between the north and south of Europe. Taking a sample of 11 northern and southern countries, Figure 2.6 shows growth in median incomes between 2005 and 2013. In 2005, the difference between the poorest and richest states – Austria and Portugal, respectively – was 8,958 (PPS). In 2013, Austria and Greece now represented the two end poles of prosperity in the north and south, yet the difference in incomes between the poles has expanded to 11,838: an increase of 32 per cent. On incomes as with GDP, the EU is far from converging: rather, structural divergence characterises the economic trajectory of post-crisis Europe.

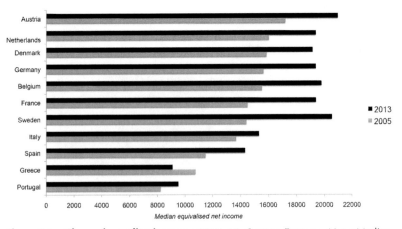

Figure 2.6   Change in median incomes: 2005–13. *Source*: Eurostat. *Note*: Median equivalised income (purchasing power standard).

LABOUR MARKETS

The greatest structural divergence in Europe today is not in GDP growth or incomes, however, but in employment opportunities and labour markets. The Europe 2020 strategy, announced in 2010 as a successor to the Lisbon agenda, has a headline target of getting 75 per cent of 20–64 year-olds into work across the EU. This is an ambitious objective, but progress towards the goal up to 2008 was positive, when an average employment rate across member states of almost 71 per cent was reached. A large element of this improvement was due to the significantly higher labour market participation rates of women and the over-55s. Between 2002 and 2008, the employment of women in the EU-27 rose from 58.1 per cent to 62.8 per cent. Since 2008, however, the employment rate of women has slightly reversed, declining by 0.2 per cent in 2012–13. In overall terms, there has been a sharp decline in employment participation since 2009 across the EU which has yet to recover, and Europe's overall participation rate remains stagnant six years on from the crisis.

National experiences of employment participation are, of course, hugely divergent. It is through the prism of employment and labour

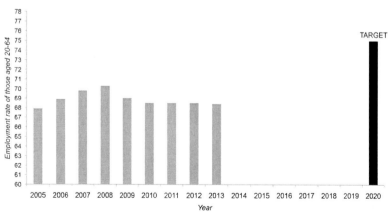

Figure 2.7   Labour force participation rates and the Europe 2020 target. *Source*: Eurostat. *Note*: Labour force participation rates of 20–64 year-olds.

markets that the heterogeneous impact of the crisis in Europe becomes starkest. As a result, the Europe of 2015 looks very different from the Europe of 10 years ago. Figure 2.8 maps labour force participation rates in the EU, demonstrating the sheer scale of inequality in employment rates ranging from a low of 53 per cent in Greece to a high of 80 per cent in Sweden. Furthermore, these two extremes symbolise the emergence of two distinct labour market blocs. The highest labour market participation rates are concentrated in a north-central bloc of Denmark, Germany, the Netherlands and Sweden, where they have risen to over 75 per cent of the labour force. In contrast to this successful core there is, with the exception of Cyprus, a southern and eastern bloc – alongside Ireland – where participation rates in 2013 all fell below 65 per cent.

The labour market situation in Europe is a different reality to that which existed before the crisis. Figure 2.9 shows the unemployment rates of 14 countries in both 2005 and 2013. In 2005, Germany had the highest unemployment rate among the selected 14 states. Remarkably, by 2013 Germany had the second lowest rate within the same group of countries, experiencing a reduction in unemployment of six per cent since 2005 despite the crisis. Greece, Spain and Cyprus, however, saw unemployment rocket during the same time period: by 18, 17 and 11 per cent respectively. The extremely low unemployment figures for Germany are an integral part of the

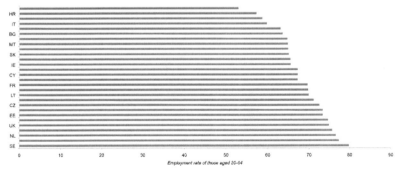

Figure 2.8 EU-wide variation in employment of those aged 20–64. *Source:* Eurostat.

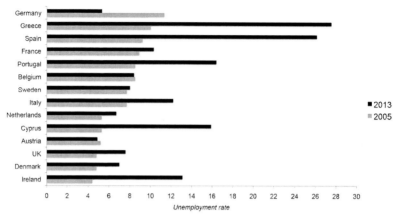

Figure 2.9   Unemployment rates: 2005–13. *Source*: Eurostat.

country's economic success during the past five years, in which Germany appears to have transformed itself through the renewal of its industrial base: from a relatively high unemployment labour market to one that is increasingly buoyant.

LIVING STANDARDS AND THE GENERATIONS

A further dimension of post-crisis Europe is demography and the variable impact of the crisis on different age cohorts. The living standards of older people have been largely protected and, in some instances, have continued to improve despite the crisis, as the result of discretionary policy choices by governments. Explanations for the relatively protected position of pensioners vary, ranging from the higher propensity of older people to vote, to welfare state 'path dependency': these constitute substantial obstacles to reform of existing pensions' systems. Since 2005, employment rates for older workers have risen year-on-year: from 42 per cent in 2005 to 50 per cent in 2015, bucking the trend in overall participation rates seen in Figure 2.7. Furthermore, the increase in the employment of older workers is an almost uniform trend across Europe. Only three countries – Cyprus, Ireland and Portugal – have seen the

Table 2.10   Percentage change in the employment rate of older workers: 2005–13

% change		% change		% change	
Germany	18	France	7.1	Sweden	4.2
Netherlands	14	Czech Rep.	7.1	Lithuania	3.8
Slovakia	13.7	Estonia	6.9	UK	3
Poland	13.4	Greece	6	Slovenia	2.8
Austria	13.1	Finland	5.8	Denmark	2.2
Bulgaria	12.7	Hungary	5.5	Romania	2.1
Italy	11.3	Latvia	5.3	Spain	0.1
Belgium	9.9	Croatia	5.2	Ireland	−0.3
Luxembourg	8.8	Malta	4.3	Cyprus	−1.0
				Portugal	−3.5

Source: Eurostat.

participation of older workers in the labour market decline. Northern European states have continued to perform well in this regard, while some eastern European examples – such as Bulgaria, Poland and Slovakia – equally stand out as success stories on this measure.

For older people not in work, relative living standards have also improved. Figure 2.11 shows both the change in the median income of the over-65s and changes in pensions spending between 2005 and 2012–13. In most European countries, the median incomes of older people have continued to grow despite the crisis. A large determinant of that growth is also illustrated in the graph; in most countries, expenditure on pensions has continued to increase relative to other public spending priorities. While social spending has been reduced in many areas of the welfare state, especially on benefits for people of working age, expenditure on pensions has been protected in many EU countries. Only four have reduced their spending on pensions since the crisis: Germany, Hungary, Poland and Sweden. This indicates that the observed differences in the position of older people do not follow a pattern of regional divergence: indeed measured by their relative position, pensioners in Cyprus, Greece, Ireland, Portugal and Spain have done well – among the most improved in Europe.

It is important to note, however, that this is a relative improvement, largely due to the extremity of cuts in other parts of the welfare

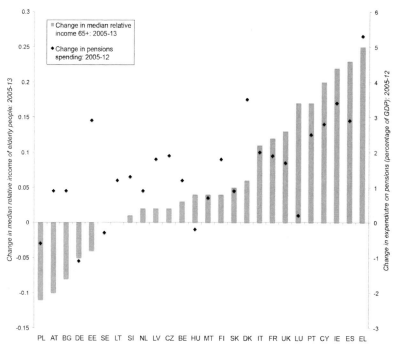

Figure 2.11 Changes in the median incomes of older people and pensions spending in Europe: 2005–12/13. *Source*: Eurostat.

state.[12] There are also major variations in the living standards of those of pensionable age: women over 60 in single households remain especially vulnerable to poverty, as are those whose private pensions offer an inadequate retirement income – a situation exacerbated by the downturn in equity markets in the wake of the 2008 financial crisis. Furthermore, reforms to public pensions systems in southern European countries will reduce the value of pensions to those now approaching retirement age. In Greece, for example, not only have the retirement ages been raised but, additionally, pensions in the future will be calculated from average lifetime pay rather than the more generous final salary indexation.

The evidence concerning the living standards of older people raises a major political question about post-crisis Europe: whether the distributional positions of particular social groups have been prioritised over others. The relative strengthening of the living standards of older people in Europe has occurred alongside a simultaneous decline in the life-chances of young people and families with children. However, the new regional political economy of Europe ensures that for young people in southern Europe, life prospects are very different to those in the north.

The divide in the life-chances of young people is at its starkest in the contrasting experiences of Germany and Greece. As part of its 'jobs miracle', the commitment to labour market reforms and an enviable high-quality apprenticeship system, Germany achieved a reduction in youth unemployment of eight per cent between 2005 and 2013. Such is the achievement of Germany in providing jobs for young people that in 2013 the German government launched a scheme to attract those under 25 from the rest of Europe to participate in its lauded apprenticeship programme. This is another world from the experience of Greece, where austerity has hit the youngest most severely: a staggering 36 per cent more Greeks under the age of 25 are out of work than was the case before the crisis. In both Greece and Spain, a young person is more likely to be unemployed than in work: a terrifying development that risks the creation of a crisis-scarred 'lost generation' in southern Europe.

Figure 2.12 highlights the emergence of distinct labour market blocs that characterise Europe's economic geography. In the largest sphere on the right are countries that combine high youth unemployment rates of over 30 per cent with relatively high 'NEET' (not in employment, education or training) rates of around a fifth of young people.[13] In these countries – which span the west to east of Europe's southern coastline – young people face a double penalty: not only are many currently unemployed, but they are not in structured education or training, as such, they face a long-term erosion of their labour market prospects. Just behind this worst affected bloc of countries – again, drawn mostly from the south and east – are another group experiencing worrying levels of youth exclusion. In the bottom left of the graph are countries not too distant geographically but worlds away in their labour market realities. These include

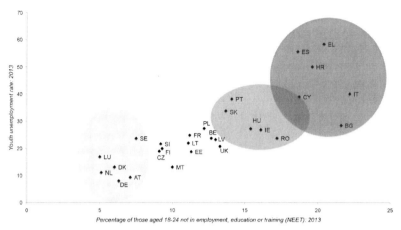

Figure 2.12   Youth unemployment and 'NEET' rates in the EU: 2013. *Source:* Eurostat.

Austria, Germany, the Netherlands and Denmark – where youth unemployment and NEET rates are extremely low at present. In the worst-performing countries even highly skilled graduates have suffered badly since the crisis. In Greece, the graduate employment rate has fallen by 13 per cent since 2005, although many other countries have maintained relatively high levels of graduate employment throughout the crisis. The marked decline in opportunities for the young in southern Europe is signifying the emergence of a new wave of migration in Europe, as young people from Greece, Italy and Spain cross the continent in search of work. As Table 2.13 demonstrates, in the UK alone the number of national insurance registrations issued to citizens from Greece, Spain, Italy and Portugal rose by a rate of 3–5 times between 2006 and 2013 for each country. This is creating tensions in the countries to which young people migrate, as populist, anti-immigrant parties thrive. This same exodus may be the harbinger of vast skills shortages in future in southern countries. National statistical agencies in Italy, Portugal and Spain estimate that over 130,000 young people have left each country respectively since the start of the crisis in 2008.[14] The scale of youth exclusion in the south is creating a further phenomenon, in which young migrants

Table 2.13   Number of national insurance number registrations in the UK from southern Europe: 2006–13

	2006	2007	2008	2009	2010	2011	2012	2013
EL	3249	3649	2931	2751	3260	5598	7417	9891
ES	9654	11836	11777	14281	19858	30020	38075	51729
IT	11060	15742	16462	16876	18464	24891	26605	44113
PT	9696	12039	12983	12211	12064	16347	20443	30121

Source: ONS (2015), *Statistical Bulletin: National Insurance Number Allocations to Adults Entering the UK*, London: DWP.

from these member states return to their former colonies – such as Angola and Brazil in the case of the young Portuguese – in the hope of a better economic future. In response to the youth crisis, the EU has adopted a European-wide Youth Guarantee programme in which all those under the age of 25 and out of work are guaranteed a job or training. Yet the figure devoted to implementing the Youth Guarantee – €6bn – is, according to the International Labour Organisation, way below what is needed to seriously tackle the scale of youth unemployment in today's Europe.[15]

SUMMARY

The impact of the crisis on the economies and labour markets of the EU has inevitably been heterogeneous, leading to a further divergence in living standards across Europe. At one end of the spectrum the UK has experienced a deep stagnation since the financial crisis, with 2013 median incomes comparable to those in 2005. That said, the UK Office for Budgetary Responsibility (OBR) recently reported that it expected living standards to rise up to 2020, although questions remain about how evenly the gains will be spread across the income distribution.[16] Meanwhile, Germany has forged ahead – increasing median incomes significantly and simultaneously achieving very low rates of unemployment – while surrounding states, such as Denmark, the Netherlands and Austria, have continued to thrive.

The situation in the south of Europe is worlds apart, as incomes stagnate and, in some instances, fall below pre-crisis levels, while rates of joblessness have rocketed to previously unheard of levels, particularly among young people. As a result, the pre-crisis ambition of European economic convergence has stalled and, in some instances, gone into reverse. The uneven impact of austerity has imposed a horizontal line across a new, economically divided, post-crisis Europe.

NOTES

1. European commission (2014), *European Economic Forecast: Autumn 2014*, Brussels: European commission.
2. Fratzscher, M. (2014), *Die Deutschland-Illusion: Warum wir unsere Wirtschaft überschätzen und Europa brauchen*, Munich: Hanser.
3. Taylor, P. 'No More Blue Banana: Europe's Industrial Heart Moves East', *Reuters*, 15 March 2015, http://uk.reuters.com/article/2015/03/15/uk-eu-industry-analysis-idUKKBN0MB0AI20150315.
4. GDP per person is measured in purchasing power standard (PPS), which corrects for price differences between countries. Consequently, the PPS makes it possible to estimate valid cross-national comparisons of the purchasing power of individuals and countries, cancelling out differences in the cost of goods and services.
5. English-speaking (UK; Ireland); continental (Austria; Belgium; France; Germany; Netherlands); Nordic (Denmark; Finland; Sweden); southern (Cyprus; Italy; Greece; Malta; Portugal; Spain); east-central (Czech Republic; Hungary; Poland; Slovakia); Baltic (Estonia; Latvia; Lithuania); south-east (Bulgaria; Croatia; Romania). The grouping of the EU's member states in this way is derived from the literature on the European varieties of welfare capitalism. Esping-Andersen (1990) suggested three models of welfare capitalism, reflected in the English-speaking (liberal), continental (corporate-conservative) and Nordic (social democratic) regimes above. Since Esping-Andersen's influential account, academics have posited the existence of further, distinct regimes in Europe. These include a southern model, see Ferrera, M. (1996), 'The Southern Model of Welfare in Social Europe', *Journal of European Social Policy*, 6(1):17–37; a Baltic model, see Toots, A. and Bachmann, J. (2010), 'Contemporary Welfare Regimes in Baltic States: Adapting Post-Communist Conditions to Post-Modern Challenges', *Studies of Transition States and Societies*, 2(2):31–34; and a relatively successful east-central model compared to a weaker, developing south-eastern model, Fenger, H. (2007), 'Welfare

Regimes in Central and Eastern Europe: Incorporating Post-Communist Countries in a Welfare Regime Typology', *Contemporary Issues and Ideas in Social Sciences,* 3(2).

6. ONS (2015), *Gross Domestic Product Preliminary Estimate, Q4 2014,* London: Office for National Statistics.

7. ONS (2014), *An International Perspective on the UK: Labour Market Performance,* London: Office for National Statistics.

8. ONS 2014.

9. Institute for Fiscal Studies (2015), *Living Standards: Recent Trends and Future Challenges,* London: IFS.

10. Taylor 2015.

11. Median incomes are calculated in PPS and as disposable incomes, giving an indicator of how much income households have to spend or save after taxes and other deductions. Median estimates of income are often preferred to mean estimates in order to correct for the small proportion of the population who earn extremely high incomes, which would skew mean income upwards. Furthermore, median net incomes are 'equivalised'. This means that, when calculating the shape of the income distribution, the size of a household is taken into account to reflect the level of income needed to attain a given standard of living. Households with dependent children, for example, require a higher household income to attain the same standard of living as a childless household.

12. OECD (2014), *Pensions Outlook*, Paris: OECD.

13. The term 'NEET' is used to refer to young people who are not currently in any form of employment, education or training. The emergence of 'NEETs' within public policy discourse reflects the growing disadvantages that many young people face in European societies, especially within the context of high youth unemployment.

14. See Ottaviani, J. 'Crowdsourcing Youth Migration from Southern Europe to the UK', *The Guardian,* 2 October 2014, http://www.theguardian.com/news/datablog/2014/oct/02/crowdsourcing-youth-migration-from-southern-europe-to-the-uk.

15. ILO (2013), *Youth Guarantees: A Response to the Youth Employment Crisis?,* Geneva: Switzerland.

16. See Arnett, G. 'Budget 2015: Are Households Really Better Off Than They Were in 2010?', *The Guardian,* 18 March 2015, http://www.theguardian.com/news/datablog/2015/mar/18/budget-2015-challenge-living-standards.

INEQUALITY AND POVERTY

INEQUALITY

In May 2014, Mark Carney, the Bank of England governor, issued a grave warning about the dangers of rising rewards at the top of society and the threat this posed to the legitimacy of the capitalist system.[1] This was a warning apparently heeded as billionaires and economic elites met for the annual World Economic Forum at Davos in January 2015. Unusually, the worrying scale and impact of income inequality in the industrialised countries was firmly on the agenda. This is a sign of the times in the wake of the financial crisis. No longer is income inequality the exclusive concern and priority of the ideological left; central bankers, and even some among the super-rich, are now apparently concerned by the scale of runaway rewards for those at the top as median incomes appear to stagnate or rise anaemically. While their motivations vary – ranging from sympathy with the goal of social justice to the need to 'save capitalism from itself' – there are few who claim burgeoning inequality is no longer a major issue for our societies. Inequality is now blamed for a whole range of social ills: from ill-health, crime and civil disorder[2] to economic pathologies, such as the unsustainable credit boom, that created the conditions for the crisis at the outset.[3]

In Europe, where many countries pride themselves on lower levels of economic inequality than other parts of the developed world such as the United States, the crisis has led to a sharp overall spike in inequality, particularly in the eurozone. Figure 3.1 shows changes in two measures of inequality – the Gini coefficient and the quintile ratio.[4] Between 2007 and 2008, the eurozone experienced a sharp rise in income inequality on both of these measures. Since then, inequality has continued to creep up gradually: from a Gini coefficient of 29.3 in 2005 to 30.6 by 2013.

Unlike the measures of growth, unemployment and living standards discussed in the preceding section, patterns of income inequality in individual member states point to varying national trajectories with much less clear regional divides. There is no straightforward geographical divergence between the north and south: the problem of inequality – and the extent to which it is successfully being tackled – varies country by country across Europe.

As such, some of the high-performing countries identified in the previous section have experienced significant increases in income inequality since 2005. These include Denmark, Germany and Sweden where, despite income growth and low levels of

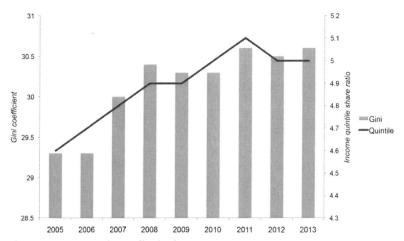

Figure 3.1   Income inequality in the eurozone: 2005–13. *Source*: Eurostat.

unemployment, the gap between the rich and poor has widened. This is a particular concern for the Nordic countries, where low income inequality is viewed as central to garnering support for generous welfare states but where, crucially, inequalities have grown at a faster rate than many other countries since the 2000s. According to the Organisation for Economic Co-operation and Development (OECD), this has been driven by the increasing rewards distributed to the top 10 per cent of earners, whose incomes have raced ahead of both the middle and the bottom of the income distribution.[5]

Inequality has also spiralled in Romania and, especially, Bulgaria: for some commentators, this is the price to be paid for 'pro-market' economic reforms. However, the group of countries that have seen significant inequality reductions are a highly diverse cluster. The rapid economic growth experienced by Poland perhaps explains why inequality has fallen so far since the 2000s. Yet the UK experience – so long a European pariah characterised by high inequality rates – is significantly harder to explain. Plausible explanations might include the delayed impact of benefit cuts to the poorest groups, the stagnation of incomes in the middle class, the decline in bonuses paid out in the pre-2008 boom years to those working in financial services, and the higher tax receipts paid by those at the top. Between 2010 and 2011 in the wake of the financial crisis, the Gini co-efficient fell faster in the UK than at any point for 50 years. The Resolution Foundation reports that hourly pay fell furthest among the highest paid between 2009 and 2014 in the UK, although the trend was relatively uniform across the distribution.[6]

Equally difficult to explain are the inequality trends in the countries most damaged by austerity in southern Europe and Ireland. While Greece, Spain and Cyprus have all experienced rising inequality, Ireland and Portugal have managed to bring inequality down. Furthermore, given the scale of austerity in Greece and Spain, the change in inequality has been relatively modest in these countries, ranging from between 1.2 to 1.5 Gini points. The situation in Europe might lead to the straightforward prediction of rising inequality in

Table 3.2 Inequality change in Gini coefficient: 2005–13

	Significant Increase		Minimal Change		Significant Decrease
BG	10.4	HR	0.9	BE	−2.1
DK	3.6	LV	−1.0	CZ	−1.4
DE	3.6	HU	0.4	EE	−1.2
FR	2.4	MT	0.9	LT	−1.7
LU	3.9	AT	0.7	NL	−1.8
RO	3.0	SI	0.6	PL	−4.9
SE	1.5	FI	−0.6	SK	−2.0
				UK	−4.4

Source: Eurostat.

Table 3.3 Inequality change (Gini) in southern Europe and Ireland: 2005–13

	Change in Inequality
Ireland	−2.0
Greece	1.2
Spain	1.5
Italy	−0.3
Cyprus	3.7
Portugal	−3.9

Source: Eurostat.

the south and contained inequality in the north, yet this is clearly not the case. It is evidently a myth to conceptualise a Europe of high inequality in the English-speaking and southern states, and of low inequality in the north. In this context, the value of existing income inequality data – and its worth as a measure of the quality of life – also comes into question.

POVERTY AND SOCIAL EXCLUSION

Along with improved labour market participation rates, the Europe 2020 strategy aims for a Europe where fewer citizens are at risk of poverty and social exclusion, with the objective of reducing the number at risk by 20 million. In the EU-27, Eurostat data shows that the proportion of the population at risk of poverty or social exclusion has been reduced from 25.7 per cent to 24.4 per cent since 2005. Yet this is still 1.1 per cent higher than the lowest figure recorded in the past decade: 23.3 per cent in 2009. Since 2009, the number of people at risk has grown: from approximately 114 million to 121 million citizens. Like the ambition for employment participation, this is now a target in reverse.

The increase in poverty and social exclusion can be dated from 2009 in the wake of the financial crisis and the beginnings of the eurozone debt crisis. Table 3.5 shows that out of the EU-27, only the six highlighted countries have experienced reductions in the number of people at risk of poverty and social exclusion. Furthermore, only three of these countries have experienced significant reductions

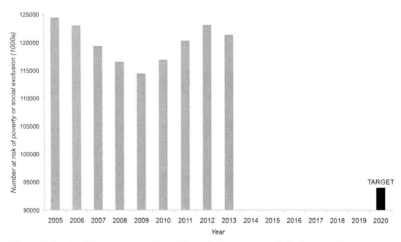

Figure 3.4   At-risk poverty and social exclusion rates and the Europe 2020 target.
Source: Eurostat.

Table 3.5   Change in the proportion at risk of poverty or social exclusion: 2009–13

	EU-27	BE	BG	CZ	DK	DE	EE	IE	EL	ES	FR	IT	CY	LV
% change	1.1	0.6	1.8	1.3	1.3	0.3	0.1	4.3	8.1	2.8	–0.4	3.7	5.3	–2.8

	LT	LU	HU	MT	NL	AT	PO	PT	RO	SI	SK	FI	SE	UK
% change	1.2	1.2	3.9	3.7	0.8	–0.3	–2.0	2.5	–2.7	3.3	0.2	–0.9	0.5	2.8

Source: Eurostat. *Note*: Data for Ireland from 2009–12.

in poverty, with the eastern member states of Latvia, Poland and Romania recording reductions of two per cent or more. The most common experience in the EU is of rising poverty and social exclusion since the crisis. Importantly, the largest rises in poverty have come in the member states most affected by austerity: Ireland, Spain, Italy, Cyprus and Portugal all recorded increases of over 2.5 per cent since 2009, with a significant increase of 8.1 per cent in Greece, as welfare provision has been drastically cut back. Notably, however, other countries have not been immune from increases in poverty: Hungary, Malta and the UK have also seen large and expanding poverty rates.

In addition to increases in the overall risk of poverty, southern Europen member states and Ireland have experienced increases in severe material deprivation and a growth in child poverty significantly above the EU average. Table 3.6 shows that this is particularly significant in Greece where the number of children at risk of poverty has risen by 12.1 per cent since 2005. In contrast, over the same period severe material deprivation has increased far more slowly in the north, with no change in the Netherlands, small increases in Denmark (+0.6) and Germany (+0.8), and overall reductions in severe deprivation in Finland (−1.3) and Sweden (−0.9).

While the common experience in the EU is of rising poverty rates, the scale of the rise has led to an intensification of the regional divides indentified in the previous section. Table 3.7 shows the

Table 3.6 **Change in the proportion of children at risk of poverty or social exclusion and overall severe material deprivation: 2005–13**

	Child Poverty (% change)	Severe Material Deprivation (% change)
Greece	12.1	7.5
Spain	3.6	2.1
Ireland	3.2	4.7
Italy	4.3	6.0
Portugal	2.8	1.6
EU-27	−0.4	−1.2

Source: Eurostat.

proportion of EU populations at risk of poverty and social exclusion. The highest poverty rates are concentrated in the south-east of Europe, yet high poverty rates as a whole curve around the continent from Europe's north-east to the south-west. The lowest levels of poverty are to be found in northern and western Europe, although there are notable exceptions in eastern and central Europe: the Czech Republic and Slovakia, for instance, both have poverty rates below 20 per cent; with much lower levels of median wages, on relative measures of poverty, these countries do reasonably well.

These findings are underlined in a paper by Zsolt Darvas and Olga Tschekassin for the Bruegel thinktank in Brussels.[7] The authors conclude: 'While the fall in severely deprived elderly people is a highly welcome development, more children were severely deprived even in 2013 than in 2007, which is worrying.' They also emphasise the sharp differences between countries in their experience of rising material deprivation: 'Before the crisis, material deprivation was very high but declining in the member states that joined the EU in 2004–07. During the crisis, there were major increases in the Baltic states after 2008, and after 2010 in the three euro-area programme countries (Greece, Portugal and Ireland) and in Italy and Spain. In the other EU15 countries there was only a minor increase and even a slight decline in central and eastern European countries. These developments suggest that the east-west divide has narrowed, while the north-south divide has widened with the crisis.'

Table 3.7 EU-wide variation in those at risk of poverty or social exclusion (proportion of the population)

Continental	English-speaking	Nordic	Southern	East-central	Baltic	South-east
BE 20.8	IE 29.5	DK 18.9	HR 35.7	CZ 14.6	EE 23.5	BG 48.0
FR 18.1	24.8	FI 16.0	ES 27.3	HU 33.5	LV 35.1	HR 29.9
LU 19.0		SE 16.4	IT 28.4	PL 25.8	LT 30.8	RO 40.4
NL 15.9			CY 27.9	SI 20.4		
AT 18.8			MT 24.0	SK 19.8		
			PT 25.3			

Source: Eurostat.

SUMMARY

Europe faces common challenges in combating inequality and poverty. Inequality as a whole is rising within the eurozone, and there is no region in Europe that is wholly exempt from these trends. States such as Denmark, Germany and Sweden, which are otherwise high performers in terms of economic growth and employment rates, have experienced rising inequality since 2008. On poverty and social exclusion, the vast majority of EU countries have also seen poverty risks increase since the on-set of the financial crisis. As a result, the objective of the Europe 2020 strategy to reduce the number of citizens at risk of poverty by 20 million looks set not to be met.

That said, Europe was divided in relation to poverty and inequality well before the crisis. Yet trends on poverty have been significantly worse in more austerity-hit countries, especially Greece. This has widened the increase in poverty rates across Europe, despite the efforts most member states have made to contain such an increase. Along with the harsh facts of falling incomes and declining employment rates, the increased risk of poverty in many southern states is another crucial factor accounting for the vast movement of people to countries elsewhere in Europe with all of the political and social ramifications that rapid migration entails.

NOTES

1. Carney, M. 'Inclusive Capitalism: Creating a Sense of the Systematic', *Bank of England*, 27 May 2014, http://www.bankofengland.co.uk/publications/Pages/speeches/2014/731.aspx.
2. See Wilkinson, R. and Pickett, K. (2009), *The Spirit Level: Why More Equal Societies Almost Always Do Better*. London: Penguin.
3. See O'Farrell, R. (2011), *ETUI Policy Brief: European Economic and Employment Policy*, Brussels: European Trade Union Institute and Lansley, S. (2012), *The Cost of Inequality: Why Economic Equality is Essential for Recovery*, London: Gibson Square.
4. The Gini coefficient is a scale of 0 to 100, where 0 represents a hypothetical society of perfect equality and 100 a hypothetical society of perfect

inequality. The quintile ratio (also called the 20:20 ratio) compares the proportion of income received by the top 20 per cent in society compared to the bottom 20 per cent. Both measures of income inequality are calculated *after* tax and benefits are accounted for.

5. OECD (2011), *Divided We Stand: Why Inequality Keeps Rising*, Paris: OECD.

6. Whittaker, M. (2015), *Time to Catch Up? Living Standards in the Downturn and Recovery*, London: The Resolution Foundation.

7. Darvas, Z. and Tschekassin, O. (2015), *Poor and Under Pressure: The Social Impact of Europe's Fiscal Consolidation*, Brussels: Bruegel.

EDUCATION AND HEALTH

Europe has historically enjoyed among the best-funded and most high-performing public services in the world. The long-term impact of the crisis is further transforming systems of public service provision in Europe, however, as budgets are constrained and demands rise in the face of changing demography and new technologies, particularly in the fields of health and education. There are some who question whether existing arrangements for delivering public services can survive, and whether there will have to be a further phase of radical institutional reform across Europe. The debate about the sustainability of European welfare states was well underway before the crisis: with the fiscal pressures on many member states having increased as a result of the crisis, the debate is set to intensify further.

EUROPE 2020 TARGETS ON EDUCATION

Along with its targets on employment participation and poverty risks, the Europe 2020 strategy aims for two specific objectives in education. Those were first proposed by the Barroso Commission in 2010 and then endorsed by the European council and parliament:

1. A reduction in the rates of early school leaving to 10 per cent in the EU.
2. At least 40 per cent of 30–34 year-olds completing tertiary level education.

In the context of a youth unemployment crisis in many EU member states, the early school leaving target has taken on enhanced significance. Young Europeans are increasingly at risk of joblessness and social exclusion; ensuring that more young people stay on at school for longer is seen as a key protective measure as that group seeks to make a smooth transition into the labour market, training or further education.

On this indicator, there is generally positive news across Europe. Despite the economic crises, the early school leaving rate has been reduced year-on-year since 2005, with Europe set to achieve the target of reducing the rate to an average of 10 per cent across the EU (Figure 4.1). Indeed, many countries have now long surpassed the 10 per cent target, while only Spain, Italy, Malta, Portugal and Romania have rates above 15 per cent.[1] This indicates a degree of diversity amid the overall positive trends in Europe, with the UK

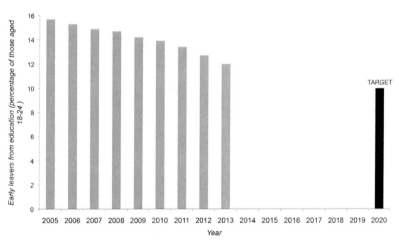

Figure 4.1   Early school leaving rates and the Europe 2020 target. *Source*: Eurostat.

unusual in experiencing an increase in early school leavers between 2005 and 2013 of 0.5 per cent. However, even in those countries where school leaving rates remain relatively high, significant progress has been made since 2005: Portugal, for example, has reduced its early school leaving rate by 19.4 per cent, while Malta has done so by 12.2 per cent. Table 4.2 shows that since 2005, only three countries have experienced increases in the early leaving rate – Poland, Slovakia and the UK; while important to note, these are nevertheless extremely small changes at less than one per cent.

Similar progress has been made on the EU's tertiary education target of 40 per cent completion for all 30–34 year-olds. The proportion of Europe's population completing tertiary education increased significantly by just under nine per cent since 2005. In 2013, 37 per cent of 30–34 year-olds in Europe had completed tertiary education, with the 2020 objective on course to be achieved. Again, many countries have already reached the target, with some member states – including Ireland, Lithuania and Luxembourg – surpassing 50 per cent tertiary participation. Significant challenges remain, however, for some member states, with a varying range of countries – as diverse as the Czech Republic, Italy and Austria – with less than 30 per cent of citizens completing tertiary education. There are major challenges for those countries that lag behind the more successful performers. Austria and Germany's labour market model is far more dependent on vocational education and training than the 'mass participation' higher education model of member states. Countries such as Germany and Austria retain a significant manufacturing sector and are characterised by corporatist

Table 4.2   Change in the proportion of early school leavers: 2005–13

	EU-27	BE	BG	CZ	DK	DE	EE	IE	EL	ES	FR	IT	CY	LV
% change	−3.8	−1.9	−7.9	−0.6	−0.7	−3.6	−4.3	−4.1	−3.5	−7.4	−2.5	−5.3	−9.1	−4.6

	LT	LU	HU	MT	NL	AT	PO	PT	RO	SI	SK	FI	SE	UK
% change	−2.1	−7	−0.7	−12.2	−4.3	−1.8	0.3	−19.4	−2.3	−1.0	0.1	−1.0	−3.7	0.8

Source: Eurostat.

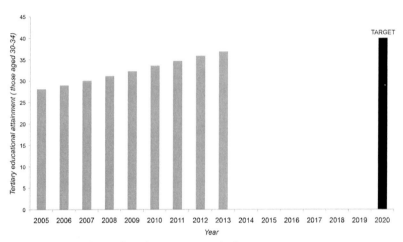

Figure 4.3 Tertiary education targets and the Europe 2020 target. *Source:* Eurostat.

arrangements with a high level of co-ordination between government, employers and trade unions – all conducive to maintaining
high-quality vocational training systems.

Nevertheless, although some states have far more advanced
tertiary education systems than others, progress within the EU as
a whole has been marked. Table 4.4 shows that all countries in the
EU-27 have achieved increases in tertiary education completion
since 2005. Countries from across all European regions have made
notable improvements, including those in austerity-hit countries
such as Ireland (13.4 per cent), Greece (9.6 per cent) and Portugal
(12.5 per cent). However, the endemic weaknesses in the southern
labour markets means that many of those who successfully complete higher education must look elsewhere in Europe for work.
The dilemma for these countries is whether to invest in higher
education expansion when many graduates are likely to migrate
elsewhere.

Europe's achievements in education buck the trend when compared to the problems many countries have experienced with
inequality and poverty, as well as the more rapid decline in living

Table 4.4   Change in the proportion of those completing tertiary education: 2005–13

	EU-27	BE	BG	CZ	DK	DE	EE	IE	EL	ES	FR	IT	CY	LV
% change	8.9	3.6	4.5	13.7	0.3	7	12.0	13.4	9.6	2.4	6.4	5.4	7	22.2
	LT	LU	HU	MT	NL	AT	PO	PT	RO	SI	SK	FI	SE	UK
% change	13.6	14.9	14.0	8.4	8.2	6.8	17.8	12.5	11.4	15.5	12.6	1.4	10.7	13.0

Source: Eurostat.

standards experienced in Europe's austerity-hit southern periphery. However, austerity itself may account for some of the improvement in reducing the early school leaving age: with fewer job and training opportunities, increasing numbers of young people might decide to stay on at school to improve skills and qualifications. Unless that growing number of young people who stay on at school have access to jobs and opportunities, it is not clear that the drive to reduce the early leaving age alone will be of benefit.

A similar debate also emerges regarding the utility of mass higher education in countries with high rates of youth unemployment. A valid question is the extent to which higher education is appropriate for young people who are otherwise destined to endure poor labour market prospects. There is also a question of quality in terms of the relationship between formal educational attainment and actual skill levels. OECD work suggests that literacy scores for individuals with tertiary education vary considerably between member states.[2] This reflects a wider problem of basic literacy skills. While overall there is less inequality in literacy scores according to educational attainment levels between Europe and America, mean literacy scores within the EU differ widely between member states: in Italy and Spain, for example, the mean literacy score is some 10 per cent below that in Finland, the Netherlands and Sweden.

Furthermore, the advances made in tertiary education participation are largely due to policy changes and expenditure plans put in place long before the financial crisis. It will not be clear until the end of the decade whether or not tertiary education participation

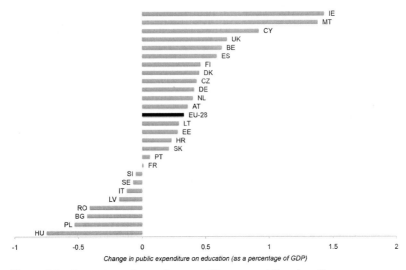

Figure 4.5   Percentage change in expenditure on public education as a proportion of GDP: 2005–11. *Source*: Eurostat.

rates – akin to incomes and living standards – have been significantly affected by the downturn. Figure 4.5 shows that, at least until 2011, the majority of countries continued to invest in education. Between 2005 and 2011, only eight countries – six of which are in eastern Europe – had reduced the amount that governments spend on public education. Notably, increases were highest in some of the most crisis-hit countries such as Ireland, Cyprus and Spain. However, more recent figures, drawn by Bruegel from the Eurostat database of general government expenditure by function, point to a more troubling picture of post-crisis developments (Table 4.6).

Public spending in education has been reduced significantly between 2009 and 2012 in the crisis-hit countries: by seven per cent in the Baltic states, 10 per cent in Italy and Spain and 14 per cent in Greece, Portugal and Ireland. In the same period, expenditure rose by five per cent in the rest of the EU15 and by eight per cent in the other central and eastern European countries. OECD research has demonstrated no clear relationship between spending on education

Table 4.6 General government expenditure by function, percentage change 2009–12 (in current prices and constant exchange rates)[3]

| | Share | | Percentage Change in Current Prices. 2009–12 | | | | |
| | | | Greece, Ireland, Portugal | Italy, Spain | 10 Other EU15 | Baltics | 10 Other CEE |
	EU28	EU28					
Total general govt expenditure	100	4	−12	1	6	−3	7
Interest payments	5	23	14	32	19	164	22
Broad services	17	−2	−12	−11	2	−15	−1
Economic affairs	9	−5	−45	5	−6	−20	−4
Environment protection	2	−5	−26	−8	−4	−6	21
Health, recreation	17	4	−20	−7	8	−6	12
Education	11	2	−14	−10	5	−7	8
Old age	20	10	0	8	10	15	13
Family and children	4	0	−19	−10	3	−14	1
Housing	1	12	−30	6	13	23	20
Unemployment	4	0	11	14	−5	13	−11
Sickness and disability	6	7	−7	−1	9	−5	12
Other social protection	5	7	−11	5	9	26	8
Memorandum: inflation		8	6	8	7	12	10

Source: Bruegel using Eurostat data.[4]

as a proportion of GDP and educational outcomes.[5] For all that, if this trend were sustained in the medium term, it would be remarkable if the divergences in educational attainment and skills capabilities that are already a critical factor affecting competitiveness did not widen.

HEALTH AND WELLBEING

A major indicator of quality of life and social wellbeing is health. Europe has had one of the healthiest populations in the world in the postwar era, with infant mortality rates significantly below, and life expectancies significantly higher, than are the case in the United States. Nonetheless, one of the most important measures of health – life expectancy at birth – shows significant variation across the EU. In general, the highest life expectancies for men and women are found in western Europe, with Spain achieving the highest female life expectancy of 85.5, and Sweden the highest male life expectancy of 79.9. At the other end of the scale, eastern Europe has the lowest levels of life expectancy: 77.9 for women in Bulgaria and 68.4 for men in Lithuania (Table 4.7). Similarly, for subjective wellbeing – an increasingly popular measure of social progress – Europe also displays a parallel divide.[6] Average life satisfaction in Europe varies from a high of 8.0 in the Nordic countries to a low of 5.4 in the south-eastern Europe.[7] On both these objective and subjective measures of health and wellbeing, Europe is overwhelmingly divided between its east and west rather than its north and south. Furthermore, longitudinal data from the European Social Survey show that of the two southern countries for which data are available – Portugal and Spain – average life satisfaction has been unchanged since 2008, indicating that economic factors might have a less significant impact on happiness levels.

Despite significant health inequalities in Europe, countries in the east have made significant progress over the past decade. For the life expectancy of men – where the divide is far larger between the west and east compared to that of women – the biggest gains in life expectancy since 2005 have been achieved in eastern Europe.

Table 4.7   Highest and lowest female/male life expectancy: 2012

Highest Female Life Expectancy	Lowest Female Life Expectancy	Highest Male Life Expectancy	Lowest Male Life Expectancy
Spain – 85.5	Bulgaria – 77.9	Sweden – 79.9	Lithuania – 68.4
France – 85.4	Romania – 78.1	Italy – 79.8	Latvia – 68.9
Italy – 84.8	Hungary – 78.7	Spain – 79.5	Bulgaria – 70.9
Luxembourg – 83.8	Latvia – 78.9	Netherlands – 79.3	Romania – 71.0
Finland – 83.7	Lithuania – 79.6	Luxembourg/UK – 79.1	Estonia – 71.4

Source: Eurostat.

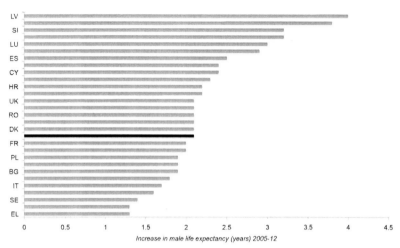

Figure 4.8   Change in male life expectancy: 2005–12. *Source*: Eurostat.

The four largest increases in male life expectancy up to 2012 were in Latvia, Estonia, Slovenia and Lithuania (Figure 4.8). Such progress is notably high; in Latvia, for example, where male life expectancy increased four years in just one seven-year period. Each country in the EU saw male life expectancy rise between 2005 and 2012. However, some countries might be expected to have performed better. Poland, for example, given its buoyant economy, saw male life expectancy increase by just 1.9 years. The evidence is that it takes more than economic growth to boost life expectancy, including investment in public healthcare and action to reduce unhealthy behaviours.

According to the OECD social expenditure database, health expenditure in Europe has remained relatively stable during the crisis, though the Bruegel paper referred to above suggests a more worrying picture. Health spending in Greece, Portugal and Ireland was 20 per cent lower in 2012 than it was in 2009. It was seven per cent lower in Italy and Spain. At the same time it grew by eight per cent in the rest of the EU15 and 12 per cent in central and eastern European member states (apart from the Baltics).

However, as with education, it is unlikely that such data reveals the full extent of how the crisis has affected health outcomes. The consensus of public health experts, typified in David Stuckler and Sanjay Basu's critique of austerity policies' health effects, *The Body Economic*, is that the crisis has led to a major rise in health problems in austerity-hit countries, including suicide, depression and infant mortality.[8] In Greece, for example, the crisis has been linked to a rise in HIV infections and malaria.

SUMMARY

On education, the EU is moving successfully towards meeting the Europe 2020 targets of reducing the number of early school leavers and increasing those achieving tertiary level qualifications. On health, large inequalities continue to exist between Europe's east and west, although increases in life expectancy have been strongest in countries such as Latvia, Estonia and Slovenia.

Nevertheless, on both health and education, the true impact of the crisis is in all likelihood not yet fully apparent in existing official EU data. It will take some time, for example, to determine whether the crisis has affected tertiary education attainment or had an effect on life expectancy trajectories. Epidemiological evidence points to a number of health crises in European states, particularly in those such as Greece, where the effects of austerity have been most acutely felt. This will continue to pose significant challenges to Europe's public health and education systems.

NOTES

1. Early school leaving rates are below 10 per cent in: Czech Republic (5.4); Denmark (8.0); Germany (9.9); Estonia (9.7); Ireland (8.4); France (9.7); Croatia (4.5); Cyprus (9.1); Latvia (9.8); Lithuania (6.3); Luxembourg (6.1); Netherlands (9.2); Austria (7.3); Poland (5.6); Slovenia (3.9); Slovakia (6.4); Finland (9.3); and Sweden (7.1).

2. OECD (2014), *Education at a Glance 2014: OECD Indicators*, Paris: OECD.

3. Belgium, Croatia, Slovakia and Romania are not included because of lack of data; data reported for the aggregate of the remaining 24 countries of the EU (EU24). 10 other EU15: Austria, Belgium, Denmark, Finland, France, Germany, Luxembourg, Netherlands, Sweden and United Kingdom. Baltic states: Latvia, Lithuania, Estonia. 10 other central and east European states: Bulgaria, Croatia, Czech Republic, Hungary, Poland, Romania, Slovenia, Slovakia, Cyprus and Malta. For the Baltic states, the 2008–12 period is shown, because fiscal consolidation started earlier in these countries. The aggregates for countries with different currencies were calculated using constant exchange rates (the average of 2009–13) and therefore exchange rate fluctuations do not affect the values shown. Broad services include: general public services except interest payments, defence, public order and safety and community amenities.

4. Table 2 from Darvas, Z. and Tschekassin, O. (2015), *Poor and Under Pressure: The Social Impact of Europe's Fiscal Consolidation*, Brussels: Bruegel.

5. OECD (2014), *Education at a Glance 2014: OECD Indicators*, Paris: OECD.

6. See Legatum Institute (2014), *Legatum Prosperity Index*, London: Legatum Institute.

7. European Social Survey 2012.

8. Stuckler, D. and Basu, S. (2013), *The Body Economic: Why Austerity Kills*, London: Allen Lane.

POLITICS AND CULTURE

This chapter examines the impact of changing social realities in Europe on society and politics. In particular, it considers whether the economic pressures and austerity which are increasingly dividing Europe may, in turn, be fomenting the growth of populist parties on left and right which represent a fundamental challenge to the established political order of postwar Europe.

THE RISE OF POPULISM

The previous sections of this report indicate that the Europe of 2015 is increasingly divided and that the traditional engine of European convergence has gone into reverse. The risk is of an ever-more polarised Europe which is drifting apart, calling into question the basic tenets of the political project of European integration. On the one hand, there is the old division between east and west. Eastern Europe remains a considerably poorer region than western Europe, while life expectancy rates still appear to be from different continents. Yet, on many measures, eastern European countries have had a 'good crisis'. Income and economic growth has been strong in places, especially Poland, while many states show signs of 'catching up' with the west on health and education.

On the other hand, there is the re-emergence of an old division –
between north and south among original member states – which, in
the run up to the crisis, had long been assumed to be shrinking as
a result of a process of economic integration driving convergence.
Instead, the years of convergence between the north and south up to
2008 have given way to a new divergence in Europe. Economic and
income growth, as well as measures of deprivation and poverty, have
gone in opposing directions. In western Europe, there is an increasingly successful core, centred in and around Germany, and a peripheral south, exemplified at its most extreme by the profound decline
of Greece. And, despite the impressive growth figures recorded by
the UK in the last two years, the stagnation in living standards and
productivity, if it continues, represents an important challenge to the
Anglo-liberal model of economic growth.[1] In the north of Europe
then, despite the ongoing weaknesses of the broader eurozone, there
is a case to be made that the source of economic strength and influence has shifted too: across the North Sea from the UK to Germany.
This is a structural economic shift in Germany's favour.

As the economic crisis has gradually abated, the new Europe
emerging from it is giving way to sharp and deeply worrying political developments and social tensions. The expansion of the EU to the
east, combined with the relative and in some cases absolute decline
so evident in the south, has given birth to new political forces. It has
reinforced the growth of populism that predates 2008.

Prior to the crisis, many imagined that the growth of populism
was in strong part a reaction to the *success* of European economic
integration, with the growth of tensions between its 'winners' and
'losers', often characterised in inevitably simplistic terms such as the
division between 'cosmopolitans' and 'communitarians'.

The first high-profile successes of rightwing populism were those
of the Freedom party in Austria joining a centre-right led coalition
in 1999; the Pim Fortuyn insurgency in the Netherlands in 2001,
followed by the later success of Geert Wilders's party; and Jean-
Marie Le Pen's National Front forcing the Socialist candidate,
Lionel Jospin, into third place defeat in the first round of the French

presidential election in 2002. This was followed in 2005 by the shock rejection of the draft EU constitutional treaty in referenda in France and the Netherlands, two of the founding states of the common market. Yet the consequences of the crisis have been for populism to rise to a new level, shaking the very foundations of the established party system across the south and heightening the populist reaction in the north.

Table 5.1 demonstrates how across Europe so-called populist parties rose to prominence in the 2014 European parliament elections. It is, of course, important to emphasise several points about these results. As even the European parliament's strongest admirers admit, it barely touches the lives of its electorate, even though its powers are now considerable: as a consequence, elections to the parliament are a natural vehicle for protest votes. Second, even then, about 70 per cent of the MEPs elected in 2014 can still be categorised as strong supporters of European integration – the UK is a rare exception here.

Even so, in the 2014 European parliament elections, while some parties came from the left, such as Syriza and Podemos, and others are hard to classify (for example, Italy's Five Star Movement), the vast majority of electoral gains made by populists came from the right.[2] In three major western European countries – Denmark,

Table 5.1   The rise of populist parties in the 2014 European parliament elections

Country	Party	Percentage Vote	Country	Party	Percentage Vote
Denmark	People's party	26.6	Netherlands	Party for Freedom	13.3
UK	Ukip	26.6	Finland	Finn's party	12.9
Greece	Syriza	26.6	Sweden	Sweden Democrats	9.7
France	National Front	24.9	Greece	Golden Dawn	9.4
Italy	Five Star Movement	21.2	Spain	Podemos	8.0
Austria	Freedom party	19.7	Poland	Congress of the New Right	7.2
Hungary	Jobbik	14.7	Germany	AfD	7.0

the UK and France – rightwing populists topped the popular vote in those elections.

Many of these political parties, including those on the left, derive their support from citizens who are increasingly disillusioned with the EU. The reasons for this disillusion vary whether for its purported lack of democratic accountability, its association with the free movement of labour and the link in the public mind to downward pressure on wages, or the imposition of austerity policies in southern Europe. Austerity in particular appears to have driven support for both the populist left and right in Europe. In the south, the experience of austerity has driven voters towards parties determined to scale austerity back, while many voters in the north feel they have paid too high a price for profligacy on the Mediterranean. In addition to dissatisfaction with European institutions, populists also gather support from other growing resentments closer to home: most notably hostility towards political parties of the centre left and centre right that are perceived as incapable of 'making a difference' and the domination of political life by a narrow, professionalised and technocratic political class, which in some countries is also seen as corrupt.

However, even in the southern member states most hard hit by the crisis, while there is clear evidence of massive discontent with the established party system, there is no common pattern of electoral realignment. In Greece, the national elections of February 2015 confirmed the remarkable success of Syriza, a disparate coalition of traditional far-left parties and a broader anti-austerity movement. The Panhellenic Socialist Movement (Pasok), the main governing party of the democratic left since the restoration of democracy, has virtually collapsed. Yet Syriza faces a difficult, perhaps impossible task in holding together its majority. It has to secure some relief from austerity from its eurozone partners, while at the same time meeting the strong wish of the Greek electorate to remain a member of the euro.

Italy, paradoxically, has seen the strongest rise in Euroscepticism, with the main opposition parties on the right and far left calling into question Italy's membership of the euro, together with the remarkable emergence of the anti-political establishment Five Star Movement. Yet Italy is governed by a charismatic insurgent from within the structures of the Democratic party, Matteo Renzi, who won a relatively open party primary and whose rhetoric is one of bold reform. His strength of character, mixed with optimistic expectations that his force of will can engender some economic recovery, appears for the moment to stand in the way of what could be a wider collapse of confidence in the Italian political system.

The situation in Spain is different again. The established party system is challenged as never before since the democratic transition from Francoism in the 1970s. The standing of both the centre-right Popular party (PP) and the centre-left Spanish Socialist Workers' party (PSOE) has fallen dramatically in the polls. There is a sense that the electorate blames the traditional parties as much for Spain's economic difficulties as it does Brussels for its externally imposed austerity. In this vacuum, separatism has strengthened in Catalonia, adding to PSOE's difficulties as the national party most sensitive to Catalan nationalist sentiment, but at the same time totally unwilling to support Catalan independence. Second, new challenger parties have emerged. Podemos's leadership represents a leftist, 'middle-class academic', rejection of the existing *casta* of the party system. But, at the grassroots level, it has attracted as much as 20 per cent electoral support from those radicalised by Spain's extreme austerity, particularly young *indignados* having to live with a massive rise in generational inequalities. But PSOE in Spain is not fully comparable to Pasok in Greece. Its hold on power, through the multiple tiers of Spanish democracy, reinforced by an electoral system that, for the national parliament, exhibits a two-party bias, could prove more resilient. PSOE has elected a new young leader who may be able to reassert its appeal sufficient for it to maintain its position as the first or second party of the state.

With the notable exception of Greece and Spain, however, the left in the wider EU has failed to capitalise on the crisis in the

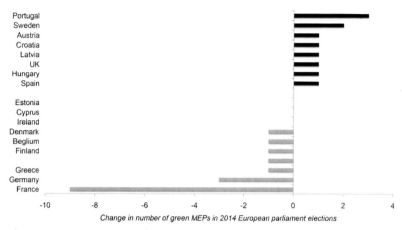

Figure 5.2   Green party performance in the 2014 European parliament elections.
Source: Eurostat.

same way as the right. This is exemplified by the performance of green parties in the European parliamentary elections. Only in Portugal were they particularly successful, with the Democratic Unitarian Coalition and the Earth party winning a combined share of the vote close to 20 per cent. This fits into the broader pattern of growth in the radical left across Europe's southern periphery. However, the wider picture of green performance in Europe has been one of stagnation. In European parliament elections in 2014, most countries saw no change in the number of green MEPs, while any gains made by green parties were cancelled out by equivalent losses.

Still, the rise of radical and populist right and left parties is fracturing the support of the traditional social democratic and conservative parties. The emergence of populists in many guises is challenging the hegemony that parties of the centre left and centre right have enjoyed in Europe since the second world war. While there are slightly more governments led by the right than the left in Europe, political parties of the centre are increasingly forced to work together in coalition governments. Only three EU states had one-party majorities at the time of writing: Malta, Slovakia and Spain.

Table 5.3   Governments in Europe: March 2015

One-party majorities	Malta (L); Slovakia (L); Spain (R).
Left-leaning coalition governments	Austria; Croatia; Czech Republic; Denmark; France; Greece; Italy; Lithuania; Luxembourg; Romania; Slovenia; Sweden.
Right-leaning coalition governments	Belgium; Bulgaria; Cyprus; Estonia; Finland; Germany; Hungry; Ireland; Latvia; Netherlands; Poland; Portugal; UK.

France might be added to this list given that the Greens have surrendered their ministerial posts in the French government, although the Socialist party appears to be affected by serious political divisions. Once considered temporary, forced responses to electoral arithmetic, 'grand' coalitions that span the two wings of the centre are seen as increasingly the norm. In coalitions led by the centre right in both Germany and the Netherlands, social democratic ministers occupy key positions of influence over policy. And, in the future, grand coalitions might be seen as fundamental in holding back the populist tide across Europe.

POLITICAL AND IDEOLOGICAL DIVISIONS IN THE NORTH AND SOUTH

The rise of radical, populist forces poses a profound challenge to Europe's traditional political parties, national political institutions and the wider EU. And while citizens in the north are increasingly attracted to the Eurosceptic, anti-immigrant parties of the right, the turn to the left by citizens in the south appears to represent a more fundamental, and widespread, malaise towards existing democratic institutions. The ire in the south is aimed at both Brussels and the perceived cooperation of national governments with the imposition of austerity.

Figure 5.4 shows the extent of feelings of trust in the EU in the continental, Nordic and southern regions of Europe.[3] In 2005, during the heady days of the economic boom, the southern countries had the

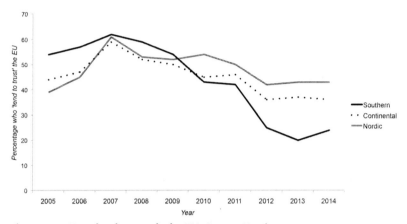

Figure 5.4   Trust levels towards the EU. *Source*: Eurobarometer.

highest levels of trust in the EU. This is unsurprising: membership
of the union and the single currency were delivering a seemingly
interminable rise in prosperity and living standards. Trust in the
EU peaked in 2007 before starting to decline in all three regions.
Yet the scale of lost trust is far greater in the southern countries.
In 2014, 43 per cent and 36 per cent of citizens in the Nordic and
continental regions trusted the EU. The corresponding figure in the
south was just 24 per cent. Meanwhile, in the UK trust in the EU
has plummeted: from a high of 36 per cent in 2007 to 19 per cent in
2013. In the UK dislike of Brussels goes along with an increasing
recognition that it might be in the country's interests to remain an
EU member, now that the prospect of an early referendum makes
this question a real choice, not simply a popularity poll. Nonetheless,
in both the UK and the austerity-hit countries, the EU faces a deep
crisis of disillusionment and mistrust.

   The decline in political trust evident in the south does not end
with the EU. As Sonia Alonso has written for Policy Network, citizens in southern Europe are significantly more concerned about the
state of democracy in their own countries, too.[4] The gap between
the southern and northern regions in terms of national democratic
trust and satisfaction has widened considerably since 2002.[5] In 2012,

Table 5.5   The trust gap in democracy between the north and south: 2002–12

	2002	2012
Trust in government (% gap between north and south)	9	32
Trust in political parties	6	25
Satisfaction with democracy	6	25

Source: Alonso (2013), derived from Eurobarometer.

for example, 32 per cent more people in the north had trust in their national governments compared to those in the south. In 2002, the corresponding difference was just nine per cent. According to Alonso, southern Europeans are experiencing a profound feeling of 'democratic breach'; where trust has remained relatively robust in the successful north, it is on the verge of collapse in the south of Europe.

The division in trust between the north and south is beginning to manifest itself in what Lluis Orriols terms a distinct 'ideological divorce' in Europe.[6] In an analysis of election manifestos, Orriols shows a quantitative shift in the ideological direction of parties in the north and south. On average, parties in Greece, Italy, Portugal and Spain (together with Ireland), have shifted to the left: supporting more expansive social policies combined with less intensive austerity and extracting some 'payback' from the financial sector for the post-2007 bailouts. On the other hand, parties in the rest of the EU have witnessed a shift, albeit slight, to the right marked by lower support for welfare spending and less tolerance of debt, deficits and high taxes. It is as if distrust of markets encouraged by the financial crisis has driven even deeper distrust towards the role of governments. This has made the political landscape increasingly inhospitable for social democratic parties. Such evidence underlines how the diverging success of the populists – the radical left in the south and the radical right in the north – is filtering through to the policy proposals of the mainstream centre. At many levels then – citizens, populists and traditional parties – post-crisis Europe is being exposed to changing political winds.

SUMMARY

The politics of post-crisis Europe is very different to that of the recent past. In the northern countries, many voters – disillusioned with the EU, immigration and the bailing out of the south – have shifted their support to the rising parties of the radical right. Populist right parties enhanced their support at the 2014 European parliament elections, with victories in the popular vote in countries such as France and the UK. In the south, the situation is vastly different. The radical, anti-austerity left has gained in prominence, with the rise of Syriza, Podemos and the success of radical, green-leaning parties in the Portuguese European elections. In these countries, traditional social democratic parties face an existential. In the rest of Europe, the greens and the radical left have failed to capitalise on the crisis, a symptom of northern Europe's underlying shift to the right.

The political scientist Peter Mair reflected on the ongoing decline of the centre in his 2013 book, *Ruling the Void,* which demonstrated how citizens had withdrawn their allegiance – and interest – from mainstream political parties. Mair contended that such parties had similarly neglected the question of citizens' democratic rights.[7] In the light of recent political developments in Europe, Mair's opening lines issue a stark warning to parties of the centre left:

> The age of party democracy has passed. Although the parties themselves remain, they have become so disconnected from the wider society, and pursue a form of competition that is so lacking in meaning, that they no longer seem capable of sustaining democracy in its present form.

There are other significant attitudinal divisions in the new politics of Europe, driven in part by differing views on the trustworthiness of political institutions and satisfaction with democracy itself. Citizens in the south are now far more sceptical than those in the north when it comes to both the EU and their national governments, something that is driving support for anti-establishment movements such as Syriza. This is accompanied by a quantitative change in the ideological character of politics in the north and south of Europe: where parties in the former have moved rightwards, those in the latter have tended to shift towards the left. This further emphasises the extent to which new political cleavages and divisions are emerging across Europe, further undermining the historic goal of long-term integration.

NOTES

1. Hay, C. (2013), *The Failure of Anglo-liberal Capitalism*, London: Palgrave Pivot UK.
2. The authors' understanding of Podemos, its commonalities and differences with Syriza, were greatly assisted by conversations with Pablo Simón of Politikon; Andrés Ortega; José Fernández Albertos of CSIC; José Moisés Martín Carretero; José Moisés Martín Carretero of PSOE; and David Mathieson.
3. Continental (Austria; Belgium; France; Germany; Netherlands); Nordic (Denmark; Finland; Sweden); southern (Greece; Italy; Portugal; Cyprus; Spain).
4. Alonso, S. 'A Perfect Storm: Europe's Growing North-South Divide', *Policy Network*, 12 September 2013, http://www.policy-network.net/pno_detail.aspx?ID=4459&title=A-perfect-storm-Europes-growing-North-South-divide.
5. Alonso defines the northern grouping as Germany, Finland, the Netherlands and Austria.
6. Orriols, L. 'The Ideological Divorce in Europe', *El Diario*, 12 June 2013, http://www.eldiario.es/piedrasdepapel/gran-divorcio-ideologico-Europa_6_142145798.html.
7. Mair, P. (2013), *Ruling the Void: The Hollowing of Western Democracy*, New York and London: Verso.

CONCLUSION

As this report demonstrates, the eurozone crisis and consequent economic fall-out has consolidated and fundamentally intensified a divide between the stronger northern economies and the weaker southern ones. At the same time, some of the former communist states in eastern Europe – particularly Poland – have continued to thrive despite the crisis, enjoying rapidly rising living standards and new-found prosperity. Europe is increasingly a continent of division: of growth versus stagnation; rising real incomes versus falling real incomes; impressive jobs growth versus markedly higher unemployment. The depth of this divide and its social and political consequences pose major questions about the future viability of the European project.

Of course, the new reality north-south polarisations should not obscure the continuing reality of social problems across the entire EU. In many member states, rich and poor alike, the crisis has deepened inequality as conventionally measured and it is not just in the south that generational inequalities have sharpened. The politics of most member states since 2008 have prioritised the needs of older voters over young people and families with children. Even in countries with high levels of employment, the problems caused by insecurity and low pay, particularly in more flexible labour markets, appear to be growing. What is new, however, is the sharp social division between north and south accentuating political tensions and cleavages.

ECONOMIC AND SOCIAL CONSEQUENCES

In recent years, one of the more notable effects of Europe's growing inequality is the migration of young people from the south to the north, with hundreds of thousands of young people from Greece, Italy, Portugal and Spain escaping the misery of rampant youth unemployment. This is driven, in turn, by the significant increase in youth exclusion, poverty and material deprivation. Meanwhile, member states from across the EU are struggling to hold back the tide of rising inequality.

The social situation in the EU is not entirely negative. As this report reveals, progress has continued towards meeting headline Europe 2020 education targets, while the generally improving position of Europe's elderly is to be welcomed. Nor should one exaggerate the bleakness of the economic picture. In many states, unemployment has remained relatively low. Countries like the UK, for example, have experienced nothing like the mass job losses of the 1980s and 1990s: rather there has been a robust growth in employment. Similarly in the eurozone, the risk of a further bank collapse and government sector debt defaults has largely subsided: overall, growth is returning, the balance of payments position is relatively strong and there has been a significant relaxation of austerity. Ireland and Spain are now enjoying steady growth and it appeared in early 2015 that even Greece could be turning the corner with the prospect of some growth and a primary budget surplus at last being achieved. A degree of post-crisis stability in Europe has been established, anaemic and conditional though it currently appears.

However, the research presented in this report reveals the extent of the rapid and steep fall in living standards in the south. This risks a permanent impoverishment of countries like Greece and Portugal, in which wages are 'reset' to much lower levels, and populations learn to live with permanently higher levels of unemployment. But, for compelling political and social reasons, the extent of such divergence is clearly unsustainable, especially given that Europe once aspired to social and economic convergence.

Referring to the unequal distribution of GDP per person across many regions of the EU, some informed observers, such as the economics commentator Paul Mason, argue that the European dream of convergence has comprehensively failed: the aim was for the wealth of more prosperous regions – from the north of Italy through to Scandinavia – to gradually disperse or 'trickle down' to the poorer south and, eventually, the east.[1] In his view, the crisis appears to have stalled this ambition, potentially sounding its death knell. While the success in central Europe, most notably of Poland, does not necessarily confirm Mason's arguments, the situation in Greece and Italy remains of great concern.

In addition, the increase in social and economic inequalities in Europe is now profoundly affecting citizens' views of European society, political institutions and the democratic mandate of their own governments and the EU. As Alonso suggests, people in the south are rapidly losing trust in governments, political parties and democracy itself.[2] This is leading to a 'new economic and territorial cleavage in Europe between north and south'. Diverging living standards are increasingly splitting Europe apart: within this context, Europe's grandest ideal – solidarity as expressed in the imprecise but nonetheless resonant goal of 'social cohesion' – is not easy to restore. The growing divide between Europe's regions is arguably the most dangerous fault line in European politics today.

POLITICAL RAMIFICATIONS

As a consequence of Europe's new social and economic divides, it is increasingly clear that there are continuing political ramifications to the crisis, with the status quo under considerable pressure from electorates everywhere. This was in evidence during the European parliamentary elections in 2014, when the nature of the political divisions were laid bare: not between social democrats and conservatives, but between a contracting core in support of the European consensus and an expanding periphery, from both the populist left and right, rallying against it. This is so substantial and significant that it can no longer be dismissed as a 'fringe'.

The rejection of the status quo reached a crescendo in January 2015 with the election of Syriza in Greece, just two seats short of an overall majority. It was elected on an electoral platform that explicitly rejected the austerity consensus, and called instead for measures to boost public spending, halt privatisation and renegotiate Greek debt. Syriza also promised to keep Greece in the euro. In addition to Greece, in Portugal, various left parties are challenging the old regime of Socialists and Social Democrats. In Spain, Podemos, now advised by the economist Thomas Piketty, along with a new centre party, Ciudadanos, presents an unprecedented challenge to the established two-party system. One strand in those southern electorates' sense of grievance is the imposition of unending austerity without, as they see it, any democratic mandate. The EU is increasingly seen as a Europe of those who dictate and those who obey. But in Spain this is overlaid by deeper frustrations with the Spanish political system and its failure, as Podemos sees it, to address the real problems affecting citizens. Podemos has gained ground as voters react against a series of corruption scandals engulfing both the centre-left PSOE and centre-right PP. While the coherence of these new movements is questionable, as is their ability – as Syriza is quickly finding out – to pursue anti-austerity policies while remaining inside the EU, they undoubtedly indicate a fundamental challenge to the established order in the south.

The rise of a new left in Europe poses a potentially existential threat to traditional social democratic parties. Driven both by the consolidation of austerity and its seeming acceptance by the social democratic centre left, voters are increasingly tempted by radical, anti-austerity movements or green parties. In Greece, the rise of

Syriza has buried the traditional social democratic party, Pasok, while the ability of the PSOE in Spain to form the next government is compromised by the transfer of large swathes of its support to Podemos. In the UK, the old certainties of the two-party, first-past-the-post system are replaced by fragmentation as the Green party picks up new recruits. In Scotland the Scottish National party has successfully positioned itself as an anti-austerity alternative to the left of Labour. Ukip on the populist right also appeals to some former Labour voters.

However, the political reaction in the north is very different to the situation in the south of Europe: in northern Europe, populism has thrived on the right. Despite the existance of important national differences, it is often united by a common hostility towards the EU and immigration. Economic and social divergence in Europe is fuelling a belief in these member states that the nation-specific values – and countries – that built European progress in the immediate aftermath of the second world war now need to be protected. In such a vision of national protectionism, there is little scope for European solidarity, multiculturalism or the free movement principles of the EU's founding treaties. Radical-right parties have successfully exploited these feelings, effectively linking their long-held political beliefs to the crisis in the EU, winning millions of votes as a result.

Importantly for Europe's social democratic parties, just as they risk losing support from younger, liberal and middle-class voters to anti-austerity and green parties, there is the parallel risk that more socially conservative, working-class voters will change their allegiances to the populist right. Nowhere is this phenomenon more in evidence than in countries like France and the UK, where the anti-immigration National Front and Ukip look to exploit the growing disillusionment in blue-collar communities. Political scientists Matthew Goodwin and Robert Ford call this the problem of the 'left behind': citizens who would traditionally have voted for the centre left but feel excluded by globalisation, and are poorer as a consequence of the crisis.[3]

In addition to the political consequences for social democrats, the rise of both forms of populism is heightening explicit social tensions across the EU, with the resurgence of divisive cultural stereotypes such as the 'prudent north' and the 'profligate south'. Such cultural stereotypes are propagated by those who oppose ever-closer union on the grounds that unity within an incompatible Europe of differing norms, culture and values is an impossible and unrealistic dream. Here, southern Europe is conceptualised as a dangerous 'other': deviant, corrupt, backward. Cultural differences in Europe are harder to ignore – and easier to exploit – when economic and social fissures exist alongside them. The policy approach of euro bailouts and austerity leaves many northern Europeans feeling responsible for paying the debts of the south. At the same time it leaves southern Europeans feeling powerless in their own countries and at the behest of unaccountable EU policymakers. Such divisions leave the long-term direction and nature of the European project increasingly unclear.

THE ROAD AHEAD

Yet despite the gravity of these challenges, European politicians, policymakers and researchers appear stuck. To the public, years have passed in which talk of European 'growth strategies' has come and gone; yet growth remains anaemic. In the eurozone a significant shift in policy may well be taking place. The ECB has embraced an ambitious programme of quantitative easing which is holding down borrowing costs across the euro area and has led to a significant currency depreciation that will strengthen global competitiveness. The application of fiscal rules has been eased by the European commission with a more permissive approach being adopted towards investment expenditures. And the EU has launched its own investment plan. These policy shifts have taken place without great fanfare because the politics of the eurozone dictate that Germany and other northern member states cannot be seen by their own citizens to have made 'concessions'. Numerous outcomes now seem feasible for the future of Europe. One possibility is the continuation of present arrangements and policies that, while producing short-term stability, rest on an array of economic, social and political fissures which threaten to erupt in unpredictable ways. Pro-Europeans hope that the centre holds until the prospect of sustainable economic adjustment and recovery returns. Yet while this uneasy stability endures, it simultaneously threatens to drive the divisions in Europe to such an extent that the union is threatened as a whole. The best-case scenario for the present approach is one that contains the economic and social crises engulfing the south; the worst-case is one that leads to new political crises, continued economic divergence and, perhaps, the exit of certain member states from the currency or the EU itself. At present, the latter scenario seems just as likely as the first: the buoyant southern radicals and northern Eurosceptics will not be vanquished by the present trajectory of policy.

A third possibility is one of much-needed reform and change. Mario Monti argues that restoring an economic balance to Europe will require a policy of give-and-take between the richer north and the poorer south.[4] In particular, while the south should accept the need for fiscal discipline and structural reform, the north – and especially Germany – should be willing to identify and support 'growth-friendly' public investment policies.

This first point made by Monti has often been the position of politicians and policymakers from the north. There is, they argue, a divergence in the standards of governance between the two poles of Europe, which encompasses everything from the quality of the civil service to the capability of governments to implement reforms. In addition to fixing its governance weaknesses, the south should therefore follow the German economic model of labour market reform and wage moderation which purportedly accounts for Germany's successful economic performance during the crisis.

Countering this narrative is the view that the problem lies in the approach of the north, particularly laying the blame at Germany's door, with its reluctance to support demand-side policies and stimulus measures elsewhere in the EU. This point is the argument of the radical politicians in the south who place the blame for deteriorating economic and social conditions at the door of austerity and the reluctance of the EU and the ECB to support expansionary policies. The consequences of this northern consensus can arguably be discerned in the findings presented in this report: the socioeconomic fracturing of the south and relatively strong income, employment and economic growth in the north. There is a sense that the south has been sacrificed to support a northern preoccupation – austerity and budget discipline – regardless of the economic, social and human consequences. On the other hand, the radicals of the south know their own societies need reform, which is why they rail against the established party system. But they have not, as yet, managed to convert that instinct into a coherent political programme of reform.

This divide in public and political opinion – between pro-austerity in the north and anti-austerity in the south – is imposing polarising pressures on political parties across the EU: making unity harder at the time it is needed most. Ideological currents are moving in different directions across the continent. To hold itself together, Europe might seek to reconcile these two apparently conflicting objectives: to support the reform of political economy in the south, while encouraging expansionary measures across Europe to boost consumption, investment and growth. Labour market reforms, for example, should be accompanied by meaningful job-creation programmes and higher minimum wages to protect the position of the low paid.

Monti insists that, despite the willingness of many southern member states to accept fiscal rules of the north, much-needed structural reforms have been under-prioritised. This is because structural reforms often come up against organised interest groups domestically, while EU policymakers have been overwhelmingly focused on budgetary discipline and not meaningful structural reform. This combined effect – of domestic opposition and European myopia – has resulted in a lack of structural change. The proposed solution is to reorientate EU policy towards country-specific recommendations for reform, and to couple this with mechanisms to facilitate their financing. This would be accompanied by targeting research subsidies, infrastructure funding, SME support and innovation investment at Europe's most depressed peripheral regions as a matter of urgency.[5] Such arrangements might help to promote growth and employment in struggling member states and strengthen Europe at a time when it needs it most. In this new 'grand bargain', public investment projects would have an important role to play, as the newly installed president of the European commission, Jean-Claude Juncker, has recently set out in his €315bn investment programme.

At the same time, political parties in the south – most notably Syriza – are calling for expansionary measures alongside imposed structural reforms. The implementation of quantitative easing by the ECB is evidence that the tide might be shifting in this direction, as high real interest rates in the eurozone as a whole are reduced with the aim of boosting growth and private sector activity. The introduction of QE seems to be an explicit recognition that weak growth, as well as pockets of endemic structural unemployment, is hurting the legitimacy of the EU as a political project. Anti-austerity parties in the south, such as Syriza and Podemos, inevitably feel the EU should go further to restore prosperity, arguing for the restructuring of debt, and radical social policies such as the introduction of a basic income.

A more comprehensive reform agenda needs to be developed further in order to provide a genuine alternative to austerity policies. This is not the place to set out such an agenda in detail, but the following ideas ought to be rapidly explored.

• The first point to emphasise is about the availability of national policy space given the constraints of austerity. The reality is that even in the hard-hit south, there is more room for manoeuvre at national level for a positive reform agenda than either the established parties have been able to take advantage of, or the new challengers have been able to articulate in practical terms. Public finances must inevitably remain heavily constrained, but in Greece

and Spain, for example, there is scope for tax reform and measures
to tackle tax evasion which could significantly improve public rev-
enues. Southern welfare states are notoriously inefficient in focus-
ing limited resources on those most in need, largely because of the
priority they give to pensions: a gradual shift in support to young
people and families should be feasible. Public administration and
public services are often badly run: this is not just a question of
using resources more efficiently, but also, for example, identify-
ing reforms in education that will improve outcomes and result
in qualifications that promote employability. At the same time,
active industrial policies are needed, with cities in the driving seat,
to promote innovation and entrepreneurship, while facilitating
the growth of employment-generating SMEs. How can the most
depressed regions in the EU be given a viable economic future,
by putting in place a modern industrial policy that supports investment in innovation, infrastructure and human capital? The aim
would be to promote the growth of new industries that provide the
next generation of employment opportunity. What does this mean
for state aid rules within the single market? How can structural
funds be used more creatively to promote growth?

- As this report has shown, living standards in the EU are diverging
  sharply: what more should be done to ensure minimum standards
  such as a European-wide income guarantee through a common
  minimum wage and minimum family income across the EU?
  If richer member states want to stem the flow of unskilled migration from poorer EU member states, then would it not be in their
  interests to meet part of the costs of such a policy?

- Young people in Europe have so far borne the brunt of the crisis, suffering the sharpest fall in living standards and facing the
  greatest prospect of unemployment since the crisis: the EU has
  legislate for a European employment guarantee, but what more
  should be done to advance the interests of Europe's youngest
  citizens? How can the north assist the south to better train its
  young people and close the deficit in intermediate skills? Can
  young people who have migrated to the north to acquire skills be

offered support to return to their member states and set up new small businesses?

- Migration has created renewed social tensions particularly in western Europe: how can the rights of migrant labour be protected while at the same time enforcing social standards that safeguard indigenous workers from exploitation? What is needed to prevent a race to the bottom in the EU?

- How can the EU act to prevent tax evasion and aggressive tax avoidance particularly within the financial services sector which serves to weaken the tax base of member states in ways that inhibit public investment and effective government intervention?

- The EU needs to make more effective use of existing instruments in order to promote socially inclusive policies: how can the EU budget be reformed so as to promote social investment in an era of budgetary constraint? Is there a window of opportunity to revisit the current common agricultural policy arrangements?

The risk is that the emerging divide within Europe will become a time bomb that threatens the stability of the EU's political cohesion. It could provoke electorates to support policies that, at best, threaten the EU while, at worst, risk reviving the continent's very worst memories of political extremism and intolerance. The challenge for policymakers is to defuse this ticking time bomb with policies that promote EU-wide improvements in growth, incomes, jobs and lower inequality.

NOTES

1. Mason, P. 'If Europe is to Overcome Islamist Terror, It Needs to Fight for the Values It Holds Dear', *The Guardian*, 11 January 2015, http://www.theguardian.com/commentisfree/2015/jan/11/europe-survive-islamist-terror-learn-to-fight-for-values-holds-dear.
2. Alonso, S. 'A Perfect Storm: Europe's Growing North-South Divide', *Policy Network*, 12 September 2013, http://www.policy-network.net/pno_detail.aspx?ID=4459&title=A-perfect-storm-Europes-growing-North-South-divide.

3. Ford, R. and Goodwin, M. (2014), *Revolt on the Right: Explaining Support for the Radical Right in Britain,* London: Routledge.
4. Monti, M. 'Europe's North and South Must Reform Together', *Financial Times,* 19 December 2013.
5. Taylor 2015.

APPENDIX

Statistical Definitions

SECTION 2. ECONOMIES AND LABOUR MARKETS

2.1: Actual and Predicted GDP

Gross domestic product (GDP) is a measure of the economic activity, defined as the value of all goods and services produced less the value of any goods or services used in their creation. The calculation of the annual growth rate of GDP volume is intended to allow comparisons of the dynamics of economic development both over time and between economies of different sizes. For measuring the growth rate of GDP in terms of volumes, the GDP at current prices are valued in the prices of the previous year and the thus computed volume changes are imposed on the level of a reference year; this is called a chain-linked series. Accordingly, price movements will not inflate the growth rate.

2.2–2.4: GDP per Person

Expressing GDP in PPS (purchasing power standards) eliminates differences in price levels between countries, and calculations on a per head basis allows for the comparison of economies significantly different in absolute size.

2.5–2.6: Median Incomes

Median equivalised disposable income is the median incomes of households, after tax and other deductions, that is available for spending or saving, divided by the number of household members converted into equalised adults; household members are equalised or made equivalent by weighting each according to their age, using the so-called modified OECD equivalence scale. The equivalised disposable income is calculated in three steps:

- all monetary incomes received from any source by each member of a household are added up; these include income from work, investment and social benefits, plus any other household income; taxes and social contributions that have been paid, are deducted from this sum;
- in order to reflect differences in a household's size and composition, the total (net) household income is divided by the number of 'equivalent adults', using a standard (equivalence) scale: the modified OECD scale; this scale gives a weight to all members of the household (and then adds these up to arrive at the equivalised household size):
  - ○ 1.0 to the first adult;
  - ○ 0.5 to the second and each subsequent person aged 14 and over;
  - ○ 0.3 to each child aged under 14.
- finally, the resulting figure is called the equivalised disposable income and is attributed equally to each member of the household.

The purchasing power standard, abbreviated as PPS, is an artificial currency unit. Theoretically, one PPS can buy the same amount of goods and services in each country. However, price differences across borders mean that different amounts of national currency units are needed for the same goods and services depending on the country. PPS are derived by dividing any economic aggregate of a country in national currency by its respective purchasing power parities.

PPS is the technical term used by Eurostat for the common currency in which national accounts aggregates are expressed when adjusted for price level differences using PPPs. Thus, PPPs can be interpreted as the exchange rate of the PPS against the euro.

2.7: Employment

The employment rate is calculated by dividing the number of persons aged 20–64 in employment by the total population of the same age group. The indicator is based on the EU Labour Force Survey. The survey covers the entire population living in private households and excludes those in collective households such as boarding houses, halls of residence and hospitals. Employed population consists of those persons who during the reference week did any work for pay or profit for at least one hour, or were not working but had jobs from which they were temporarily absent.

2.9: Unemployment Rate

Unemployment rates represent unemployed persons as a percentage of the labour force. The labour force is the total number of people employed and unemployed. Unemployed persons comprise persons aged 15–74 who were: (a) without work during the reference week, (b) currently available for work, i.e. were available for paid employment or self-employment before the end of the two weeks following the reference week, (c) actively seeking work, i.e. had taken specific steps in the four weeks period ending with the reference week to seek paid employment or self-employment or who found a job to start later, i.e. within a period of, at most, three months.

2.10: Employment of Older Workers

The employment rate of older workers is calculated by dividing the number of persons in employment and aged 55–64 by the total population of the same age group. The indicator is based on the EU

Labour Force Survey. The survey covers the entire population living in private households and excludes those in collective households such as boarding houses, halls of residence and hospitals. Employed population consists of those persons who during the reference week did any work for pay or profit for at least one hour, or were not working but had jobs from which they were temporarily absent.

2.11: Median Incomes of Older People/Pensions Expenditure

The indicator is defined as the ratio between the median equivalised disposable income of persons aged 65 or over and the median equivalised disposable income of persons aged between 0 and 64.

The 'Pensions' aggregate comprises part of periodic cash benefits under the disability, old-age, survivors and unemployment functions. It is defined as the sum of the following social benefits: disability pension, early-retirement due to reduced capacity to work, old-age pension, anticipated old-age pension, partial pension, survivors' pension, early-retirement benefit for labour market reasons.

2.12: Youth Unemployment/NEET Rates

For youth unemployment, see 2.9 definition.

The indicator young people neither in employment nor in education and training (NEET) provides information on young people aged 15–24 who meet the following two conditions: (a) they are not employed (i.e. unemployed or inactive according to the International Labour Organisation definition) and (b) they have not received any education or training in the four weeks preceding the survey. Data are expressed as a percentage of the total population in the same age group and sex, excluding the respondents who have not answered the question 'participation to education and training' and in change over three years (in percentage points). Data comes from the European Union Labour Force Survey.

2.13: National Insurance Registrations (UK)

The DWP National Insurance data covers people allocated a National Insurance Number (NINo) for all types of work – including the self-employed and students working part-time – and whatever the length of stay in the UK. It also covers adult overseas nationals allocated a NINo to claim benefits or tax credits. In addition, the data is a 100 per cent sample held at case-level data sources.